AMBER WAVES OF GRAIN

AMBER WAVES

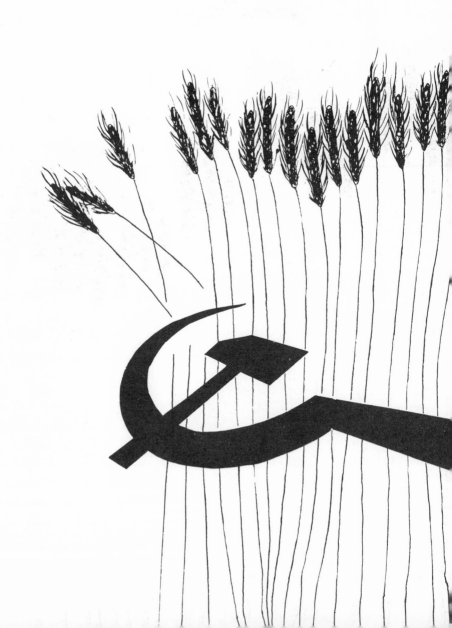

OF GRAIN

James Trager

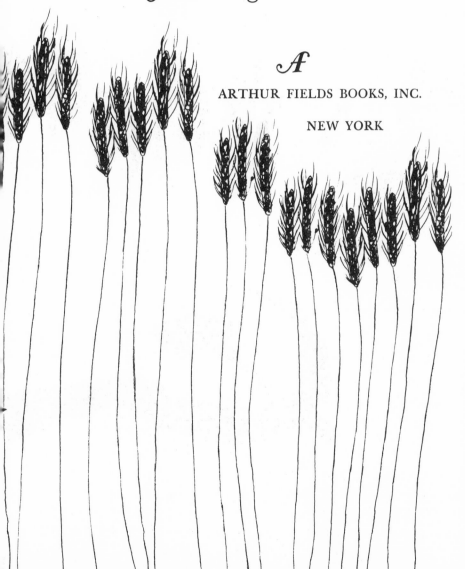

A

ARTHUR FIELDS BOOKS, INC.

NEW YORK

BOOKS BY JAMES TRAGER

The Enriched, Fortified, Concentrated, Country-Fresh, Lip-Smacking, Finger-Licking, International, Unexpurgated Foodbook

The Big, Fertile, Rumbling, Cast-iron, Growling, Aching, Unbuttoned Bellybook

Amber Waves of Grain

Library of Congress Cataloging in Publication Data

Trager, James.
    Amber waves of grain.

        Bibliography: p.
        1. Wheat trade—United States.   2. United States—Commerce—Russia.
    3. Russia—Commerce—United States.
    I. Title.
    HD9049.W5U58   382'.41'3110973   73-78971
    ISBN 0-525-63010-4

Published simultaneously in Canada by Clarke, Irwin & Company Limited, Toronto and Vancouver
SBN: 0-525-63010-4
Library of Congress Catalog Card Number: 73-78971
Designed by The Etheredges

For Chie

ACKNOWLEDGMENTS

Morton Sosland started it all. Morton is a college classmate, first encountered in days when guns came before
butter and none of us ate margarine. As years went by,
I found myself increasingly interested in matters of food
and nutrition, with a growing awareness of food's vital significance in human history, in domestic politics, and in
foreign relations. When I ran into Morton Sosland again,
he was editor-publisher of the key trade journal in the
breadstuffs industry and I had just published *The Foodbook*. A year later, while I was finishing *The Bellybook*,
Morton received some mysterious transatlantic phone
calls that involved him in a strange intrigue of global
dimensions, a political-economic phenomenon that was to
have immense effect on food prices in America and abroad.
Talking to Morton about the 1972 grain sales to Russia,
I saw they vividly demonstrated the importance of food
and food prices in a world still torn between guns and
butter.

Another classmate is Arthur Fields, who appreciated
the significance of the secret hotel room grain deals pulled

off in the summer of 1972. Arthur realized they were more than simply record size commercial transactions; he provided the necessary encouragement; and he edited the manuscript to good advantage.

Before there was a manuscript there had to be spadework, and here I had the help not only of Morton Sosland and his people at *Milling & Baking News,* in Kansas City, especially Melvin Sjerven, but also in varying degrees the cooperation of major export houses, the U.S. Department of Agriculture, and other government agencies and private companies.

Because the story of the Russian grain raid has become so politicized, many of the sources I consulted offered sharply divergent views. Some were involved in pending litigation. The information received was evaluated in light of these factors.

Murray S. Aboff, Managing Editor of *Supermarket News,* Edward F. McDermott, Editor of *Food Merchants Advocate,* and Frank Packer, of Supermarkets General Corp., Woodbridge, New Jersey, were good sources. So were Lawrence O'Brien of ITT-Continental Bakeries; Nelson Chang and Morris J. Markovitz of Hayden, Stone, Inc.; Chester W. Keltner of Keltner Statistical Service, Kansas City; Michael C. Jensen of *The New York Times;* and Dr. John A. Schnittker of Schnittker Associates, Washington, D.C. (Dr. Schnittker was undersecretary of agriculture in the Johnson administration).

Among present Agriculture Department officers and personnel, I am grateful to the following for their patient assistance: Charles W. Cobb, Claude Freeman, James J. Naive, A. Donald Seaborg, and James Vermeer of the Economic Research Service; Wayne F. Dexter of the Office of Management Service; and William R. Randolph and Glenn W. Tussey of the Export Marketing Service.

Edward W. Cook of Cook Industries, Inc., Memphis, was the most informative of the export people. Also co-operative were W. B. Saunders and Thomas Connally of Cargill, Inc.; James Bowe of Carl Byoir & Associates, who is on full-time assignment to Cargill; Sheldon L. Berens of Continental Grain Co.; and Philip A. McCaull of Louis Dreyfus Corporation.

Edward Kimmel of the Bureau of International Commerce, Department of Commerce; Frederick Larsen of the U.S. Maritime Administration in the Commerce Department; and Ms. K. D. Hoyle of the Bureau of Labor Statistics, U.S. Department of Labor, also supplied valuable help in some complex areas.

Not all of these people will agree with all the views expressed in the book; none is responsible for any errors it may contain.

*La destinée des nations dépend de
la manière dont elles se nourrissent.* . . .
—BRILLAT-SAVARIN

1.

An older generation called it dough, the new one called it bread, but money by any name was buying less food in America. And U.S. housewives were hopping mad.

They had been complaining for years. No subject comes closer to home than the price of food, none arouses more emotion than the amount and quality of food a dollar buys at the supermarket. But in 1973 the cries of protest grew louder and uglier.

In Greenvale, Long Island, the Pathmark supermarket, one of 100 in a six-state area running south from Massachusetts, is a focal point for communities from miles around, not because it is open twenty-four hours a day six days a week but because its prices are so low. But even at Pathmark meat prices had been going up a few pennies each week for months, and when customers arrived on Monday morning, Lincoln's Birthday, they found new prices posted. Meat and poultry items were now higher by 10 cents, 20 cents and even more per pound than they had been the week before.

Pathmark's meat market is big and depersonalized;

most of the meat is packaged in plastic and the butchers are closed off behind a big plate-glass window. The Long Island women were not to be put off by any of that. They were indignant. They were screaming. They demanded an explanation.

The manager who came out to mollify the crowd had been briefed at a meeting of all Pathmark meat department managers.

Why were meat prices so high?

He gave them the party line straight from Pathmark headquarters at Woodbridge, New Jersey.

"It's the Russians," he explained. That was the big factor. They bought all that grain, you know. It pushed up feed prices, and feed accounts for 65 to 80 percent of a meat producer's cost, so. . . .

Supermarket prices had been going up by fractions of a penny each month throughout 1972; by the end of the year they had increased an overall 5 percent, according to the Bureau of Labor Statistics, though meat had gone up 14 percent and fish 11 percent.

The 5 percent figure for 1972 looked like peanuts when the 1973 figures came out.

Food prices are a major component of the Consumer Price Index (CPI), computed by the Bureau of Labor Statistics because many labor contracts contain automatic cost-of-living increase provisions pegged to the Index (government pensions rise by the same criteria). Since its inception in 1913, the CPI has undergone four revisions —a fifth is now underway—and by the end of 1976, the Index will include prices of more convenience foods to reflect changes in U.S. eating habits.

Few convenience foods are now included in the Index. The ninety-six food items whose prices were checked by paid volunteers in 1,500 chain, local, and "mom-and-pop" grocery stores across the country in 1972 and 1973 were selected on the basis of how often these foods appeared in the shopping carts of urban wage earners surveyed in 1960 and 1961, breadwinners who made a maximum of $6,220 a year after taxes if they were heads of families, $3,560 if they were single. (Purchasing habits of farm workers, and of more affluent business and professional people who buy so many convenience foods, were not represented.)

Food items used to compute the CPI include bread, cereals, meats, vegetables, dairy products, and candy. The only canned soups included are bean and chicken; the only frozen foods are orange juice and lemonade, breaded shrimp, five kinds of fish, and broccoli. Not on the shopping list are such favorites as peanut butter, canned peaches, and all cheeses except American process cheese. Also left out are crackers, pizza, potato chips, and all spices and condiments except pickle relish.

Foods in the Index bounded a startling 2.3 percent in January, 1973, above their levels in December. (The meat, poultry, and fish group spurted 3.3 percent). Even after eliminating seasonal factors, the 2.3 percent rise was the sharpest one-month increase in twenty-two years. And the January rise was followed by rises of 2.4 percent in February and 3.1 percent in March. At the rate they were going, and little was being done to reverse their direction, food prices would be up nearly 30 percent within a year.

The March jump surpassed the record of January, 1951, when food prices had vaulted 2.5 percent, but that was during the Korean War inflation. This was peacetime, or at least trucetime. How could food prices have shot up so much more in just three months of 1973 than they had in all of 1972?

Meat, poultry, and fish prices took even bigger hops

than did food prices in general. So did wholesale prices of farm products, feed, and processed foods; they climbed at a rate of well over 50 percent, a grim portent of things to come at grocery stores and supermarkets.

Worried that prices would rise even higher, Americans were buying more cars, more houses, and more appliances than ever in the first quarter of 1973. The Gross National Product (GNP), even discounting inflation, was rising at a healthy 8 percent annual rate. That looked like prosperity, at least on paper.

But for most Americans, food was the single largest cost of living. And food was getting costlier every day.

Dr. Earl L. Butz, the secretary of agriculture, had been saying that Americans pay "not for the high cost of living but for the cost of living high." Americans, he said, spent less than 16 percent of their spendable income on food.

Not all Americans lived so high. "It makes us shudder" when he uses that figure, an Agriculture Department economist said. "The trouble is, it lumps the Rockefellers in with the welfare cases."

Only when after-tax income reached the elite heights of $17,125 a year for a family of four, including two schoolchildren, did what the USDA called a "liberal" food budget of $228.40 per month drop to Butz's 16 percent of the family's spendable income.

Many American families in 1973 had more than two schoolchildren and disposable incomes of less than $6,000 a year. Some things they could put off buying, but food was not one of them.

It was poorer families, and people on fixed incomes, who bore the brunt of the food price increases. Among these people, nutritional deficiencies went up along with food prices.

To make ends meet, more Americans shopped for specials, used cents-off coupons, switched to cheaper cuts of meat, substituted more beans, cheese, eggs, and poultry for red meat, and even turned flower gardens into vegetable gardens, like the Victory Gardens of World War II. Some staged boycotts on meat. Some bypassed supermarkets to buy staples and produce at food cooperatives, food warehouses, and other wholesale outlets where they purchased flour, rice, and sugar in twenty-five- and fifty-pound bags, picked their own produce straight out of packing cases, and bagged their own purchases. Many joined buying clubs of ten or more families with similar tastes in food and shared the jobs of buying food staples at wholesale markets, distributing the food, and keeping simple books.

Still, only a tiny minority was willing or able to make so radical a change in its food buying habits.

Most Americans bought at the supermarket. Bought more pasta and less meat, maybe, but they bought at the A&P and at Acme. They wheeled their shopping carts down the aisles of Allied and Arden-Mayfair, of Colonial and Finast. They lost their children in the labyrinths of First National and Fisher, of Food Fair, Giant, and Grand Union. They compared the prices stamped on cans and boxes at I.G.A. and at Lucky, at Jewel, and at Kroger. They waited in the checkout lines at National, at Pathmark, at Piggly Wiggly, at Pueblo, and at Safeway. They paid their money and handed over their food stamps to the checkout clerks at Shopping Bag and Shop-Rite, at Stop & Shop and at Winn-Dixie.

And they wondered how in the world some Russians buying U.S. grain could have such a stunning impact on the prices they paid at the register.

2.

New York City on a long summer holiday weekend empties out like a bottom-ripped flour sack. The streets are eerily empty, the city's voice a faint echo of its workaday roar.

July 2, 1972, was a Sunday, a rare day with a high in the low 80s and a good breeze to keep the air shining clear.

One of the few notables in town this perfect day was grandmaster Bobby Fischer, the U.S. chess champion. He was not supposed to be in New York. He was supposed to be in Reykjavik, Iceland, where his title match with Soviet grandmaster Boris Spassky was scheduled to begin that afternoon. But Fischer was delaying the start of the match with prima donna demands for more money.

At the New York Hilton there were plenty of vacancies. What guests there were tended to be jazz enthusiasts, in town for the nine-day Jazz Festival held in previous years at Newport, Rhode Island.

When two Midwestern types checked in for a stay of uncertain length, nobody paid much attention. Nobody could have dreamed what a stunning effect these out-of-town buyers would have on American lives.

But anyone mystified by the sudden, unexplained leaps and bounds in U.S. food prices will have to turn back to that perfect summer day for at least part of the answer.

For the two visitors at the New York Hilton were from Moscow, not Cedar Rapids. And they were about to buy up a quarter of the entire 1972 U.S. wheat crop. And great quantities of barley, corn, oats, rye, and soybeans as well.

They bought it all stealthily, digging deep into Soviet gold reserves to do it.

Why? What is the larger significance of this gigantic, unprecedented purchase, not only for American consumers but for the whole world?

And who was "John Smith," the still unidentified tipster who somehow had better information on the Russians than anyone else but the Soviet purchasing agents themselves?

Wheat is Earth's single most important food crop, occupying close to a quarter of the world's croplands. The largest grower of wheat by far is the Soviet Union. From 1967 to 1971, the U.S.S.R. raised an average of 90 million tons of wheat a year; Russia was an important wheat exporter.

The United States in those years, although growing nearly 120 million tons of corn to Russia's 10 million, averaged only 41 million tons of wheat. Americans, however, use only 14 million tons of wheat a year for food and 7 to 8 million for seed and livestock feed, so the United States, with some 20 million tons to spare, is the world's largest wheat exporter. From 1967 to 1971 it exported about 18 million tons a year to Russia's 6 million. America has been a big wheat exporter since Civil War days. Wheat prices in America rose to an incredible $4 a bushel then, and Northern housewives saw food prices soar. But while Southerners starved the Union exported wheat to drought-stricken Europe; the United States ever since has been supplying much of the world with the stuff of bread, noodles, chapati, macaroni, pancakes, waffles, rolls, and pastry.

In most years America competes with Russia in the export wheat market, but in 1972 the U.S.S.R. surprised the world by importing wheat. A lot of wheat. More wheat than any nation in history had ever bought before —roughly 20 million tons. And the Russians bought most of their wheat from the United States, which sold more wheat than any one nation had ever sold in a single year.

No two countries, in fact, had ever negotiated such large commercial transactions. But the deals were not made between countries over polished embassy conference tables. They were made in nondescript hotel rooms by Soviet buyers with private American and foreign export companies. And they were shrouded in secrecy.

Had the purchases taken place out in the open market, the price of wheat would have gone through the roof (as it later did) and the Russians might not have been able to buy nearly so much as they did. Had it all been done openly, consumer protests might have stopped it long before it reached the proportions it did. And Americans might have been spared some part of the higher prices they were later to pay for food.

Underlying the Soviet need for grain in 1972 was a fifty-five-year history of Russian hunger for better living standards.

More than once in history revolutions have been related to bread shortages. In eighteenth-century France, working-class people, lucky to get 250 days of work a year and ill-paid for fourteen to sixteen hours of labor, lived mainly on bread, which took at least 60 percent of their wages. A rise in the price of bread after a calamitous drought triggered the French Revolution. The Russian Revolution began when housewives in wartime Petrograd (now Leningrad) wearied of waiting in endless breadshop queues and demonstrated in protest. They were joined by factory workers, and then by Czarist troops and sailors who stormed the Winter Palace of the Romanovs.

Consumer interests were of major concern to the Paris commune; white bread, the bread of the aristocracy, became the bread of the people—nutritionally lacking but gustatorily irresistible. To the Bolsheviks, consumer creature comforts were of small matter. And the nation's food situation went from bad to much worse.

When food is scarce, prices rise. In the fall of 1970, food prices rose so high in Poland that people rioted in the streets. The Kremlin was jolted by those riots. Leonid I. Brezhnev and Aleksei N. Kosygin saw new dangers in the Soviet Union's chronic shortages of animal protein foods (the average Russian eats 95 pounds of meat and poultry per year, as compared with 237 pounds for the average American), and they embarked on a program of enlarging and improving Soviet livestock herds and poultry flocks.

The U.S.S.R. had 102 million head of cattle, only 16 million fewer than the United States; it had 71 million hogs, some 10 percent more than the United States; and its 140-million-head flock of sheep completely dwarfed the U.S. flock of 18 million. The Soviets also had 40 million more mouths to feed than America had, and its livestock did not produce nearly so much meat per animal as U.S. livestock, partly because the Russians lacked feed.

In November, 1971, Russia bought 2 million tons of U.S. corn and 1.5 million of oats and barley. The U.S. Department of Agriculture saw the purchase as a momentous breakthrough. And as a promising opportunity: the vast and growing numbers of Soviet cattle, hogs, sheep, chickens, and geese represented a huge potential for U.S. corn, oats, barley, soybeans, grain sorghums, maybe even wheat (which has a higher protein content than corn and is often used as a feed grain).

America had small surpluses of all the feed grains, though not of soybeans. Overproduction was depressing prices. Through its extension and inspection services, the USDA does act in behalf of consumers (so does the quality control section of a manufacturing firm); but since its main obligation is to the farmer, it viewed the development of new export markets in terms of firming prices at home. Higher prices for U.S. feed grains and soybeans would win the thanks—and the votes—of U.S. farmers.

If in the process of increasing America's agricultural exports the USDA's Export Marketing Service set in motion a chain of events that hiked the American housewife's weekly food bill, that was hardly the USDA's business.

Any expectations of massive feed grain exports to the Russians had to be tempered with some sobering realities. U.S.-Soviet trade in general was hardly booming; prospects for any marked increased were dampened by an overhanging disagreement about repayment of U.S. Lend-Lease aid in World War II.

After the war the United States wrote off $1.3 billion in war matériel, including food, which it had supplied to its Soviet allies; but it asked repayment of $1.3 billion for civilian goods still in use.

The Russians balked. They had paid with lives and privation in common cause with America against the Nazis, they said; they countered with an offer of $170 million. After some years of negotiation, talks broke down in 1960 and were not resumed until April, 1972, when the two sides met in Washington. They met again in Moscow in May, when President Nixon was there visiting the Kremlin; but although the United States had reduced its demand to $800 million and the Soviets had upped theirs to $300 million, the gap was still wide. And the Russians were asking for 2 percent interest terms over thirty years, the same terms given the British; the Americans insisted on 6 percent interest. Moscow also wanted Export-Import Bank credits and the same "most favored nations" tariff treatment given to Poland, Yugoslavia, and most other nations.

While the issue remained unresolved, U.S.-Soviet trade was amounting to only about $200 million a year, small potatoes for the world's two richest nations. The trade balance was heavily in America's favor; to correct this imbalance, the Kremlin wanted the United States to engage in joint ventures that would exploit the untapped natural resources of oil, natural gas, and minerals in Siberia. Washington was wary of the drain on U.S. credits that such ambitious undertakings would demand, and there was still a large residue of cold war thinking that made many Americans suspicious of any program that might help the Communists.

Nevertheless, Richard Nixon, a month before his meeting in Moscow, dispatched his new agriculture secretary, Earl L. Butz, to the Russian capital. Butz was charged with trying to negotiate an agricultural trade agreement with the Soviets.

If the Russians could spend $150 million in hard currency to buy 3.5 million tons of U.S. feed grains, perhaps they could be encouraged to buy even more of America's agricultural surplus and help the nation's sagging international trade balance.

Accompanying Butz to Moscow were Clifford G. Pulvermacher, general sales manager of the USDA's Export Marketing Service, and Assistant Secretary Clarence D. Palmby.

Palmby had served in the Eisenhower administration and during the Kennedy-Johnson years he had headed the U.S. Feed Grains Council, an industry group that sponsors projects in foreign countries to encourage livestock and poultry production that may increase U.S. feed grain exports. He returned to the USDA under President Nixon and, according to many, it was Palmby who ran the Department under Butz's predecessor, Clifford M. Hardin. When Hardin resigned in the fall of 1971 to join the Ralston Purina Company, Palmby was considered in many people's opinion, including his own, the logical and best qualified successor to Hardin.

A folksy man in his late fifties, Palmby is an ex-dairy farmer from Minnesota whose "gollies" and "goshes" mask an extraordinary sophistication about the grain trade's complex technical subtleties. When Butz got the appointment to which Palmby felt entitled, the passed-over assistant secretary resolved to quit the Department.

But first came a sense of duty. Since Butz did not have the necessary technical expertise to conclude a major trade agreement, Palmby went along on the trip to Moscow in that second week of April.

Russia's minister of agriculture, the main figure with whom the American party conferred, was Vladimir V. Matskevich, a man of sixty-two with a record of outspokenness. In 1955 he had visited the Coon Rapids, Iowa, farm of Roswell ("Bob") Garst, a great friend of Nikita

Khrushchev. Five years later Matskevich expressed skepticism about U.S. agricultural methods, and specifically the methods of Bob Garst (though he visited Garst again as recently as December, 1971). This defiance of Khrushchev cost Matskevich his job for a while, and although he was close to Khrushchev on most political issues he was banished to the virgin lands of Kazakhstan, where he remained for several years before being reinstated.

Matskevich, in April, 1972, flew his American visitors to the Crimea, in Russia's great Ukraine breadbasket. It was clear then that the winter (fall sown) wheat crop had been meager, but it was not apparent that half of it had been lost. In any event, although winter wheat accounts for three quarters of the U.S. crop, in Russia two thirds of the crop is spring wheat; and in April the Crimea's spring wheat was doing well, although a little more rain would have been welcome.

"We get only 432 millimeters (17 inches) of rain a year in this region," Matskevich told Butz, "and neither your capitalist god nor our Communist god can grow corn on only that much rain." (Corn and soybeans both need far more rain than wheat does; they grow best, in fact, where there is too much moisture for top quality wheat, which can grow in places that get only fifteen inches of rain.)

Butz picked up a handful of *chornozem,* the rich black earth of the Ukraine.

"You have this deep black soil," he said. "Why don't you irrigate?"

But that would cost a billion rubles, the Russian exclaimed.

"You could take it out of your defense budget," said Butz boldly.

He remembers Matskevich grabbing his arm eagerly.

"You are going to see Brezhnev? Good. That is what I tell him. You tell him, too."

(In the 1973 Soviet budget, unveiled to the Supreme Soviet on December 18, a 10 percent rise in spending for agriculture was provided, and some of the funds were earmarked for irrigation. But apparently Butz's budgetary suggestion was ignored: defense appropriations continued at their same high level.)

With all Matskevich's talk about corn, Butz and his subalterns returned from Moscow with denials that Russia was interested in buying U.S. wheat. Chances even for a large sale of corn did not appear particularly rosy; the USDA insisted that any trade be at commercial terms while the Soviets continued to press for liberal credit terms of 2 percent.

What really clouded hopes for any big U.S. grain sales to the U.S.S.R. were memories of what had happened in 1963, a year of terrible crop failure in Russia.

Before that, when rain did not fall in the Ukraine it fell in the new lands of Kazakhstan, first plowed (against expert advice) by Nikita Khrushchev in 1953; but in 1963 there was general drought. Crop failures forced a wholesale slaughter of livestock, especially of hogs; there was simply not enough grain to keep the animals alive. Not until 1972 would the Soviets be able to restore their hog holdings to 1963 levels.

Even flour and groats disappeared from Soviet grocery stores in 1963. Bread was rationed, housewives bought frantically and hoarded what they could against scarcities to come. To maintain supplies and to meet its commitments to Cuba and to Communist bloc countries in Eastern Europe, Moscow dipped into its precious gold reserves to the tune of $1 billion and bought wheat, some from Australia, some from Canada.

The Canadians had had their biggest wheat crop in a decade—more than 12 million tons—and the Russians bought $500 million worth of Canada's wheat and flour, paying $1.74 a bushel for the wheat.

A Minneapolis feed grain dealer, Burton M. Joseph, heard the Russians were in Ottawa. His wife, Geri, now a contributing editor of the *Minneapolis Tribune,* was vice-chairman of the Democratic National Committee and a power in New Frontier circles. That gave Burton Joseph entrée to John F. Kennedy's agriculture secretary, Orville L. Freeman, and he persuaded Freeman that selling grain to Russia could be good for America. He proposed that a consortium of U.S. grain companies go to Canada and work out a deal with the Rusians.

Under the 1918 Webb-Pomerene Export Trade Act, designed to help U.S. companies compete with international cartels, companies prevented by the 1890 Sherman Act from colluding on domestic trade could under some circumstances get together on export sales without running the risk of antitrust actions. So Joseph assembled representatives of the major grain companies and they met with the Russians at the Chateau Laurier Hotel in Ottawa. Since not every grain trader could be represented, however, questions of antitrust violations lingered and a U.S. Department of Agriculture man, who arrived after two hours of talks, suggested that each company had better operate on its own.

In 1963 the Berlin Wall had been up only two years, the Cuban missile crisis was less than a year old, the East-West trade scene was still chilled by the cold war. Congress was bitterly divided on the issue of selling U.S.

wheat to the Communists. Not only the Russians but also the Bulgarians, Czechs, and Hungarians—unable to get wheat from the U.S.S.R.—were asking to buy American wheat.

By October the USDA, which had earlier estimated the Soviet 1963 crop shortfall at 10 percent, was saying that Soviet wheat production had dropped to just 40 million tons, 27 percent below the 55 million ton figure averaged in the previous few years. Russia would either have to buy foreign grain or impose tighter rationing. Premier Khrushchev opted for imports and had already bought about 10 million tons from Australia, Canada, and elsewhere. He was prepared to buy another 4½ million tons from the United States.

Secretary of State Dean Rusk was agreeable to a sale only if Moscow was barred from reselling grain to Cuba. German Chancellor Konrad Adenauer said any sale should be conditioned on the Russians' tearing down the Berlin Wall. West Germany, said a Soviet official, wants to bring the U.S.S.R. down "with the iron fist of hunger."

Former Agriculture Secretary Ezra Taft Benson opposed the sale, as did most other Republicans, including many whose states would benefit from a large grain sale.

Richard Nixon, defeated the year before in his bid for the California governorship, was interviewed at his New York apartment by the Mutual Broadcasting System. A grain sale to the Communists, Nixon told radio audiences, would be "harming the cause of freedom."

But President Kennedy told a news conference on October 10 that he favored selling Moscow 150 million bushels (more than 4 million metric tons) of wheat, provided it was used only in the U.S.S.R. and Eastern Europe and was shipped, where possible, in U.S. vessels. If we did not sell to Russia, said Kennedy, Soviet "propagan-

dists would exploit among other nations our unwilling-
ness to reduce tensions and relieve suffering." Soviet
leaders "would be convinced that we are either too hostile
or too timid to take any further steps toward peace, that
we are more interested in exploiting their internal diffi-
culties, and that the logical course for them to follow is a
renewal of the cold war."

To the "extent that the Soviets' limited supply of
gold, dollars, and foreign exchange must be used to buy
food," said the President, it could not "be used to purchase military and other equipment." Made through private channels for cash or short-term credit, the sale would
save the United States $200 million in storage, handling,
finance charges, and other costs imposed by mounting
surpluses. It would "advertise to the world as nothing
else could the success of free agriculture." And it would
prove Americans' willingness to help needy nations. The
Russian people would know about it. (In recent months
Moscow had quit jamming Voice of America broadcasts.)

What the Russian people heard from the Soviet press
was that a grain sale would help the U.S. economy; no
mention was made of a Soviet crop failure.

Richard Nixon, interviewed on the American Broadcasting Company's television news, predicted that the sale
would "turn out to be the major foreign policy mistake of
this administration, even more serious than fouling up the
Bay of Pigs." "What we're doing is subsidizing Khrushchev
at a time when he's in deep economic trouble. It pulls
him out of a very great hole and allows him to divert the
Russian economy into space and into military activities
that he otherwise would have had to keep in agriculture."

Other Republicans objected that the Russians would
pay less than the domestic price of wheat in America, a
price supported by subsidies; the sale, they charged, would

violate Congressional policy against selling subsidized farm products to Communist nations.

While Washington politicians argued the merits of selling wheat to Moscow, Nikita Khrushchev was balking at what he called "discriminatory conditions," including the 50–50 shipping rule.

The world rate for cargo was $12.50 a ton; U.S. shipowners were demanding over $20 a ton to ship wheat to Russia. If half the grain they bought had to go in U.S. vessels, the Russians would be paying a steep price. They were still resisting the 50–50 condition on November 22, when John Kennedy was assassinated in Dallas.

Talks broke off on November 29. Not only was Moscow refusing the 50–50 shipping terms, it was asking for credit guarantees from the U.S. Export-Import Bank. On December 17 the House voted 218–169 to prevent any underwriting of private loans for U.S. grain sales to the Soviet Union; on December 24, in an unprecedented 7:00 A.M. session, the House reversed itself by a vote of 189–158. Senator Barry Goldwater charged Lyndon Johnson with arm-twisting.

But even before President Johnson signed an appropriations bill amendment giving him discretionary authority to approve Export-Import Bank loan guarantees, Soviet buyers had agreed to buy 350,000 tons of durum wheat for $78.5 million in cash, plus $11.5 million in shipping costs.

Additional sales of wheat followed in short order, but Soviet buying intentions were frustrated by tough, flag-waving American stevedores. Even though the U.S. shipping industry said it did not have enough bottoms to carry half of a 4½ million ton grain order, the powerful International Longshoremen's Association (ILA) flatly refused to load Russian vessels unless American ships were allotted the same amount of cargo the Russians got.

Commerce Secretary Luther Hodges told a news conference that the longshoremen were coming "dangerously close" to making U.S. foreign policy. *The New York Times* called them "Metternichs of the docks."

The union boycott was finally ended in late February, 1964, but grain sales to the Soviet Union amounted to less than half what they would have been had Congress, the shipping industry, and the stevedores been more cooperative.

Opposition, it should be stressed, was based entirely on ideology and political feelings, not on any fears about the effect such large sales might have on American food prices.

Richard Nixon acted to clear the way for easier exports to Soviet Russia when he lifted the twenty-one-year-old embargo on trade with mainland China in June, 1971, an embargo that Harry S. Truman had imposed when China entered the Korean War. In lifting the embargo, the President also suspended the 50–50 shipping rule that John F. Kennedy had imposed in 1963.

In addition, acting by authority granted him under the Export Control Act, President Nixon scrapped an old rule that required special export licenses for anything sold to the Soviet Union. Validated special licenses, obtained from the Department of Commerce, still would be needed for exports to Cuba, North Korea, North Vietnam, or Rhodesia; but not for exports to China, the U.S.S.R., or other Communist destinations. For these countries, as for non-Communist countries, only a general export license was needed; exports did not have to be reported until after shipment had been made.

This change in the export license rule played a major part in enabling Moscow to buy up so much American grain in 1972 without the government knowing about it.

Moscow's way was cleared also by the maritime unions, which include the National Maritime Union, the Seafarers International Union, and the International Organization of Masters, Mates, and Pilots as well as the ILA. When feed grains were sold to the Russians in November, 1971, these unions agreed to waive their demand that American ships be allotted the same amount of cargo as Russian ships. They were swayed by two arguments. One, the Nixon administration had embarked on a ten-year program to build 300 new merchant vessels and to subsidize U.S. shipowners so they could compete with foreign lines. Two, Commerce Department men convinced the unions that their intransigence simply guaranteed them 50 percent of nothing. So although strikes, based on work-rule disputes, blocked shipment of the grain from East Coast and Gulf ports in 1971, the grain did leave from Great Lakes ports.

But it did not leave in U.S. or Soviet bottoms; it all went in vessels of British, Greek, Japanese, Liberian, or Panamanian registry.

When Butz, Palmby, and Pulvermacher went to Moscow in the spring of 1972, the cold war was thawing; prospects for U.S. grain exports to Eastern Bloc nations looked much brighter. But the 1971 sales had been entirely for cash, and the Russians were now demanding favorable credit terms. As long as they felt discriminated against, there seemed little reason to believe they would be eager to buy U.S. grain unless they had a compelling need for it.

Just how badly did Moscow need U.S. grain, and specifically wheat, in the spring of 1972? Winter crops had failed, but as many experts point out, the nation had big carry-over reserves from prior years. And it was too early to predict the major harvest to come in late summer and fall. Messrs. Butz, Palmby, and Pulvermacher pooh-poohed suggestions that the Russians would not grow enough wheat to meet their own domestic needs. But in the weeks after their visit, Kremlin policy makers may already have decided they might need U.S. wheat. Looking back at it now, some people even go so far as to suggest that Moscow's reaction to U.S. bombing of Hanoi and U.S. mining of Haiphong harbor might have been much sharper had the Russians not had one eye on U.S. wheat.

3.

For most Americans, the first inkling of a possible grain deal with Soviet Russia came on July 8. On that day, the Western White House at San Clemente announced the signing of a $750 million credit agreement with the U.S.S.R. An old 1934 law, the Johnson Act, had prohibited loans to countries in default on obligations to the United States or to U.S. citizens; but although that applied to the Soviet Union and other Eastern European countries, and had been a big issue in 1963, the Justice Department had interpreted the law to allow the financing of U.S. exports.

What was surprising about this agreement was that Moscow accepted terms it had previously called unacceptable. The Russians agreed to buy U.S. grain worth $750 million over the next three years, $200 million of it the first year. The USDA's Commodity Credit Corporation agreed to extend $500 million in credit at 6 ⅛ percent interest any time during the three-year period the Russians chose to buy. The credit was contingent on the Russians' buying grain.

No mention was made of what kinds of grain the Russians planned to buy; it was generally assumed they were interested in feed grains. Everybody at the USDA was full of smiles; hopes of many years were being realized at last: Soviet Russia was becoming a major customer for U.S. feed grains.

Nobody at the Department knew, nobody at San Clemente suspected, that the men at the New York Hilton had already bought 4 million tons of U.S. wheat plus 4.5 million tons of feed grains.

The deal was the largest single commercial transaction in history; it was made with a single private trading company; it was for cash, not credit; and it was sealed with a handshake and a toast—in vodka.

The company that made the sale on July 5 was Continental Grain Co., a firm whose origins date back to 1813, when Austria's Prince von Metternich sent his armies against Napoleonic France and Simon Fribourg moved from Metz, in France, to the town of Arlon, in Belgium, where he opened a grain business.

In 1848, Simon's son Michel made a long and perilous overland journey to the Danube valley of Bessarabia, now part of the Ukraine, with bags of gold that he traded for wheat to save his famine-stricken countrymen. Belgium remained neutral in the Franco-Prussian War of 1870, and Michel's son Arthur built flour mills in Belgium and Luxembourg. Arthur's sons Jules and René moved the firm to London in 1914, when the Kaiser's armies invaded Belgium, but five years later they were back in Antwerp doing business under the name Cie. Continentale d'Importation. America was now emerging as the major source of export grain, and in 1922 the Fribourgs opened a Chicago office under the name Continental Grain Co., which soon accounted for the bulk of the family's business.

If America has a counterpart to the Rothschilds of international banking it could well be the Fribourgs of international grain trading. Arthur Fribourg's son René was an oenophile, a member of Le Chevalerie du Testevin, a connoisseur whose collection of artifacts was valued at $3.5 million. More of a businessman was his brother Jules, a highly competitive grain trader who also bred famous racehorses for the purses at Longchamps, Auteuil, and Saint-Cloud. In June, 1940, as Hitler's panzer divisions moved on Paris, Jules gathered thirteen relatives and close friends and hustled them across the Pyrenees to Portugal. His twenty-seven-year-old son Michel, working in Continental's London office, cabled a Fribourg-owned freighter and diverted it to Lisbon, where it picked up the refugees for passage to New York.

Michel, born in Antwerp in 1913, was a Pfc in a U.S. Army intelligence unit in France when his father died in 1944. He obtained a discharge and took over the presidency of Continental Grain. A naturalized American citizen, Michel Fribourg is still chairman-president and owns more than 90 percent of the firm's stock.

Continental is probably the largest privately held company in America. It handles about 25 percent of the world's international grain shipments, owns dozens of freighters, scores of barges, and all or most of at least 100 subsidiary companies that bake bread, raise chickens, package frozen dinners, raise beef on Argentine *estancias,* operate Spanish ski resorts, produce pet food, and have important positions in real estate, construction, feed grains, and other fields. Annual sales are in the neighborhood of $3 billion.

Michel Fribourg, now a shy, courtly, silver-haired aristocrat of sixty, still has a strong Gallic accent, a reminder that he grew up in Europe and studied at the

University of Paris. Fribourg is an idealist; he has a burning, selfless desire to cement East-West political relations
through increased trade relations. He is also a consum-
mate, if unassuming, capitalist who is largely responsible
for Continental's present size and success. Since 1963 he
has been on a first-name basis with Moscow's grain buyers.
It was Fribourg who ingeniously solved the dilemma of
how to sell U.S. wheat to the Russians in 1963 in the face
of the 50–50 cargo rule that imposed such high shipping
costs.

Durum wheat, used for noodles and macaroni, was
in heavy surplus in America in 1963; the USDA was offering a huge export subsidy of 72 cents a bushel to traders
able to export some of the burdensome surplus. Russians
eat little macaroni or noodles; they were not much interested in durum wheat. But when Fribourg sent a trading
team to Moscow and offered the Russians a package that
included hard winter wheat and other grades they were
interested in, along with 350,000 tons of durum, the
Russians—after six weeks of dickering—agreed.

With its big export subsidy on the durum, Continental was able to absorb the high U.S. freight rate and offer
the Russians an attractive price, shipping included.

In 1972, when the Russians phoned Continental from
Washington's luxurious Madison Hotel on Thursday,
June 29, Fribourg was at a business meeting in Paris. He
had been in meetings for weeks; he was tired; he was
looking forward to a vacation in Spain. But when he was
reached by his New York office, the Continental nerve
center in lower Manhattan, Michel Fribourg, along with
Bernard Steinweg, his brother-in-law and senior vice-
president, Gregoire Ziv, his Russian-born customer-rela-
tions man, and some other Continental bigwigs, quickly
boarded a jet for New York.

Meanwhile the Russians had also phoned Wayzata, the Minneapolis suburb where Cargill, Inc., maintains headquarters in a sumptuous sixty-three-room French provincial chateau.

If Continental is not the largest privately held company in America, then Cargill certainly is. Cargill, too, handles about 25 percent of all international grain shipments. Cargill, too, is a great, diversified conglomerate. Called "secretive, inbred, and inconspicuous" by *Time* magazine in 1963, the firm was founded in the 1860s by Will Cargill, son of a shipmaster from Scotland's Orkney Islands. Young Will set up a small grain storage shed near a rail terminal in Iowa. Expanding with the railroads and river barges, he built an empire that his descendants have continued to enlarge. Cargill's chairman Erwin Kelm is the first Cargill chief who has not been a member of the family.

Two other trading companies received phone calls that Thursday. One was Bunge Corporation, part of Bunge & Born, the Buenos Aires-based conglomerate that handles about 20 percent of world grain shipments. The other was Cook & Company, part of the publicly owned Memphis firm of Cook Industries, Inc., once big in the cotton trade, now even bigger in grain and soybeans.

Representatives of Bunge and Cook met with the Russians at the Madison Hotel in downtown Washington on June 30; they came away empty-handed. That same Friday evening, Michel Fribourg's handsome thirty-eight-old brother-in-law, just in from Paris, arrived to confer. Bernard Steinweg was asked to submit offers on wheat and feed grains the following Monday, in New York. There would be no four-day holiday weekend for Continental.

When the Russians bought U.S. wheat at the end of

1963, Continental had supplied about half that wheat. Secretary of Commerce Luther Hodges had ruled that no firm could have more than a quarter of the Soviet business; had the Russians bought all the wheat they wanted, Continental's share would have been limited to 25 percent. But Moscow was able to buy only half the amount it intended. In addition to what it bought from Continental, Russia had bought 800,000 tons from Cargill, which offered a package, durum wheat included, similar to the one devised by Michel Fribourg. Cargill sold an additional 200,000 tons to Hungary that year.

In 1972, Cargill hoped to do at least as much business with the Russians as Continental did. On Saturday, July 1, Cargill chairman Erwin Kelm, his top trader, Walter B. ("Barney") Saunders, and the Cargill merchants for corn, barley, and wheat arrived at the Madison at 11:00 A.M.

"The Russians kept talking about corn and barley," Saunders recalled later. "When I mentioned wheat they just changed the subject back to corn."

The Cargill delegation took the Russians to lunch, but when they asked if they should remain in Washington to be available for further talks they were told they might as well go back to Minneapolis. When Saunders tried to reach the Russians the following week, they had checked out of the Madison and he was unable to find them.

Khleb is a transliteration to Roman letters of the Russian word for bread. Exportkhleb is the Soviet government agency that handles grain deals with foreign countries; normally, as its name indicates, its main business is exporting Soviet grain. Its president is Nikolai Belousov (four syllables, emphasis on the third), a tall, slim, gray-haired man of about fifty. Belousov, who speaks English with only a slight accent, had been an Exportkhleb lieutenant in 1963 at the meetings in Ottawa; now he was running the show. In the years since 1963 he had often conferred with Continental's Michel Fribourg, who made regular visits to Moscow and also met with Exportkhleb officials in other cities, pursuing his dream of increased East-West trade as a means of easing world relations.

In the summer of 1971, when U.S. feed grains had been under discussion, the Russians became obstreperous in the hotel they were occupying in Cannes on the French Riviera. When they were asked to leave, Fribourg chartered a yacht and carried on negotiations at sea. Off Corsica the yacht was hit by a gale so fierce that the ship nearly foundered. Michel and Nikolai, the capitalist and the Communist, shared an experience that gave them a bond that went deeper than a mutual interest in grain.

Accompanying Belousov to America in 1972 was Leonid Kalitenko, an Exportkhleb executive of about forty whose English is almost perfect. Also in attendance was Paul Sakun, an urbane, blue-eyed, somewhat portly member of the Soviet ministry of foreign trade.

These were not the men who concluded the credit agreement announced on July 8. That was done by a team headed by Soviet Foreign Trade Minister Nikolai S. Patolichev; the trade group included First Deputy Mikhail R. Kuzmin and A. Z. Golodobenko. But it was Belousov and his associates, including specialists who appeared at certain meetings to handle technical details, who bought the grain. They bought it, we now know, at an incredible bargain.

To understand how they got such a bargain, it must be remembered that wheat is normally a surplus commodity in the United States, and that the world wheat market is normally a buyers' market. Argentina, Australia,

Canada, the European Economic Community (EEC), and the U.S.S.R. all compete in normal years, to sell wheat in the world market. In the five years prior to 1972, Canada had exported an average of 10.3 million tons of wheat a year, Australia 7.5 million, Western Europe 6.1 million, and the Soviet Union 5.9 million. The United States generally has a wheat surplus of about 20 million tons. But since domestic price supports have made U.S. wheat more expensive than foreign wheat, the United States has had to subsidize exports with tax money. In 1964, U.S. wheat sold at $2.30 a bushel; it required a 55 cent export subsidy on No. 2 ordinary hard winter wheat, the kind America mostly exports, to enable Continental and Cargill to sell that wheat to the Russians at $1.75 a bushel, which was the world price at the time.

In 1970 and 1971 world prices for wheat had dropped. The U.S. Department of Agriculture used export subsidies to maintain a "target" price of $60 a ton, about $1.63 a bushel, F.O.B. Gulf ports, for No. 2 ordinary hard winter wheat.* This was considered a high enough price to assure a decent return to U.S. farmers who use modern agricultural methods; it was considered a low enough price to discourage countries with less advantageous climate, soil conditions, technology, and expertise from trying to grow all their own wheat.

---

* There are 36.74 bushels to a metric ton (2,204.62 pounds) of wheat. The standard bushel, adopted as a unit of measurement in Anglo-Saxon times, is the "Winchester" bushel. In the town hall of Winchester, England, not far from the cathedral, a cylinder was kept to which all bushel measurements had to conform. It was 8 inches deep, 8.5 inches in diameter, and its volume was therefore 2,150.42 cubic inches. This has always been the standard bushel in America. Great Britain and all other major nations now measure grain by the hundredweight, or quintal, using the metric system adopted by France's National Convention in 1794, after the Reign of Terror, and then by most of the civilized world. But the bushel measurement is deeply entrenched in the United States. To convert to the metric standard would be costly; failure to convert has also been costly.

If domestic U.S. wheat prices rose above the $1.63 per bushel level, the USDA paid exporters the difference so they could still sell U.S. wheat at prices competitive with foreign-grown wheat. What the exporters lost buying high and selling low they made up in subsidy payments.

The export subsidy was set each day; it was announced in Washington at 3:30 P.M. Eastern time, and normally it went up or down a penny or two, according to the market, although there was nothing automatic about that. If the price at Gulf ports dropped below $1.63 a bushel, no export subsidy was required. At higher prices, the size of the subsidy was geared to keeping the export price at $1.63, but the USDA had complete discretion in the matter.

Export subsidies had figured importantly in the U.S. wheat sales to Russia negotiated at the end of 1963; they would play a vital role in the sales made in 1972.

While Nikolai Belousov and Paul Sakun were checking into the New York Hilton on July 2, Leonid Kalitenko and A. Z. Golodobenko were visiting in Washington with Continental's Gregoire Ziv, who had just arrived there, and with Clarence Palmby.

Even before going to Russia in April, Palmby had been offered a top position by Michel Fribourg, reportedly at close to twice his $38,000 USDA salary. Using Continental executives as financial references, he had bought a $100,000 cooperative apartment on Sutton Place South. Palmby had let Earl Butz know on May 12 that he wanted to leave the government; he submitted his formal resignation on May 23 and joined Continental in New York on June 8 as corporate vice-president for market planning and development.

But Palmby and his wife still had a house in Arlington, Virginia, a Washington suburb, and it was there that he entertained the two Russians and Gregoire Ziv at lunch that glorious Sunday. Neither Ziv nor the Russians had ever been in Washington. Palmby, who had never before met Golodobenko or Kalitenko, took his guests at their request on a tour of historic points of interest in Alexandria, Virginia, and across the Potomac. The talk, Palmby later testified, was of Washington, Lincoln, and Jefferson; it never touched on grain, Soviet agriculture, or such topics.

(Palmby's testimony before the House Subcommittee on Livestock and Grains in September, 1972, left many Congressmen with the feeling that he had acted improperly; the Justice Department had the F.B.I. check conflict-of-interest charges against the new Continental executive. But whereas the Bureau found no evidence of wrongdoing, this did not persuade disgruntled farmers to drop lawsuits they had filed against Clarence Palmby, the USDA, and some of the grain export firms.)

Grain was very much the subject at the New York Hilton the next afternoon. When Michel Fribourg and his men showed up for negotiations with Exportkhleb officials, interest centered on wheat.

The cash, or spot, price of U.S. ordinary hard winter wheat, F.O.B. Gulf ports, was at that point $1.66½ a bushel, just over the "target" price. Continental owned very little wheat, although its U.S. grain elevators have a capacity of 3 million tons. If the Russians were to buy any substantial amounts, the company would have to go into the market and buy wheat to cover its contracts. It would have to assemble the wheat at coastal shipping points. There was great risk that wheat prices would rise sharply while these arrangements were being made.

What if the price went, say, to $1.77 a bushel, $65 a

ton? Would the government pay nearly 14 cents a bushel in export subsidy? Continental had to know. It had to be quite sure.

Palmby's successor at the USDA was Carroll G. Brunthaver, a professional economist with a Ph.D. who had come from Cook Industries in Memphis. When the Russians told Bernard Steinweg at the Madison Hotel on June 30 that they wanted to buy wheat, Brunthaver was the man Steinweg went to see.

Carroll Brunthaver is a tall, thin, and today extremely nervous young man of about forty who likes to remind people when he gives a speech that he served his country patriotically as a fighter pilot in the Korean War.

"They used to say the job of a fighter pilot involved 50 days of relaxation and 2 minutes of absolute hell. My job in 1972," Brunthaver told audiences in the fall of that year, "involved whole months of pure hell."

Said a USDA colleague, "Carroll is still in a state of shock." And so he appeared to be. Unlike his blustery boss Earl Butz, who unblushingly tells off-color stories in mixed company, Brunthaver is a bit of a milktoast, a man trying to do his job without making waves.

Yet the ripples from this man's decisions in the summer of 1972 would turn into tidal waves in U.S. supermarkets a year later.

On Monday morning, July 3, Continental's Bernard Steinweg caught an early plane from New York to Washington and called on Carroll Brunthaver. The Russians, he said, had shown an interest in buying American wheat. What would be the government's policy on export subsidies? Did the Department of Agriculture intend to maintain the target price on wheat? Would it continue paying the export subsidy needed to support the $1.63 per bushel target?

An intelligent answer would have required a knowledge of how much wheat the Russians wanted to buy. Brunthaver was naturally elated at Steinweg's news. A Soviet wheat buy would be good tidings for farmers. The prime job of the USDA was to serve the interests of farmers; the more wheat America could export, the better it would be for wheat farmers. Was it Brunthaver's job to look beyond that?

Under the general export license arrangement, which required a report only after cargo was shipped, Brunthaver had no way of knowing the quantity of wheat involved unless Steinweg told him. The question is, did he demand the information? Did Steinweg tell him? For that matter, did Steinweg know?

It has been alleged that Steinweg did know and did tell, but whether or not Brunthaver knew how much wheat the Russians intended to buy does not change the answer he gave Bernard Steinweg.

Would the USDA maintain the $60 a ton target price?

Of course, said Carroll Brunthaver. We've maintained it at about that level for two years. We're not about to change.

He did not say, yes, the Department will pay the export subsidy on 100,000 tons of wheat, or even on a million tons. He committed his department to pay the subsidy and he suggested no possibility of an upper limit.

Assured by Brunthaver's pledge, Steinweg returned to New York. With his brother-in-law and other Continental brass, he went to the Russians' $95 a day two-room suite at the New York Hilton and said he was prepared to talk business. And Comrade Belousov announced that Exportkhleb wished to buy 4 million tons of wheat.

It was almost as simple as that.

In addition to the wheat, Belousov ordered 4½ million tons of feed grains, although part of this order could, at Continental's option, be supplied from sources outside the United States. Most of the wheat was hard winter wheat, along with some white wheat and hard wheat from the Pacific Northwest and some durum of any origin.

Belousov led the Continental people to believe he was buying grain only from them. He cautioned everyone at the meeting on the need for absolute secrecy. Michel Fribourg and his men hardly needed to be told. If word leaked out that the company was in the market for all that wheat, prices would skyrocket. Fribourg would never be able to cover his commitments at the agreed upon prices.

4.

On the floor of the Chicago Board of Trade, "The Pit"
made famous by novelist Frank Norris seventy years ago,
fortunes still turn on scraps of information.

It may seem unconscionable, even immoral, to reap
riches because a crop has failed, because a strike has
throttled shipping, because hungry mouths outnumber
food supplies. But for every profit in a commodity trade
there is a loss. Half the winners profit not on bad news
but on good—a crop harvested before a storm, a drought
ended, a pest invasion quelled, a record yield, an increase
in planted acreage.

Traders who profit on such news are those who have
sold contracts short, anticipating lower prices that come
with abundant supplies.

The big volume of trade in futures—contracts bought
for future delivery—comes not from speculators but from
big commercial interests. A grain elevator company, when
it buys 5,000 bushels of wheat, will often sell a futures
contract. This "locks in" the sale of the wheat: if the
elevator company has no immediate buyer, the futures

contract assures it of an eventual buyer, since whoever buys the contract agrees, in the great fiction of the market, to accept delivery of 5,000 bushels.

(In practice, despite tired stories of wheat being dumped on buyers' front lawns, a buyer who has not liquidated his contract before its termination date merely receives a warehouse receipt for 5,000 bushels and can easily sell that receipt. Unless he does it quickly, though, he may be billed for storage charges.)

A miller or exporter, who must have wheat to make flour or to ship abroad, or a baker who must have flour to bake bread, may buy wheat futures if he thinks tomorrow's price (or next month's) will be higher. The profit he makes on his futures contracts will then make up for the higher cost of the wheat or flour he has to buy. Trading in futures, then, is essentially a hedging operation to protect buyers or sellers of commodities against any sharp rise or fall in the market.

Michel Fribourg could protect Continental against runaway wheat prices by buying futures contracts, but it would have to be done subtly, with the same crafty indirection Continental was using in its purchases of actual grain stocks.

When Continental signed its deals with the Russians in early July, wheat futures—and "spot" or cash, prices for wheat—were still low, as they generally are in early summer when America harvests her big winter wheat crop. Late in May, the International Wheat Council in London had forecast a record world wheat crop.

The standard 5,000 bushel wheat contract can be bought or sold on margin (earnest money) of only 5 to 10 percent. If the price of wheat to be delivered in March, May, July, September, or December goes up, the trader who has agreed to deliver wheat in that particular month (that is, sold short) must put up the difference between his original contract price and the actual market price; a 5 to 10 percent price rise can wipe out his stake— his broker will liquidate his contract unless he puts up more margin.

If the price of wheat goes down, the trader who has agreed to accept delivery in a given month (bought long, that is) still has a commitment to pay the price in his original contract; again, a 5 to 10 percent price drop can wipe out his stake—his broker will ask for more margin and will liquidate the account if he does not get it.

In each case, the margin payment lost pays the trader on the other end of the contract who bet the price would move the other way.

Looking at the market more positively, a 5 to 10 percent price move can double a trader's money, and in a fast moving market that can happen overnight. But commodities trading is so much riskier than stock market trading that George Goodman, who wrote *The Money Game* and *Supermoney* under the pen name "Adam Smith," said in the latter book that when he felt like trading in commodities he lay down until the feeling went away. The possibilities of large, quick profits nonetheless lured as many as half a million Americans into the commodities market in 1972. In June, most who traded in wheat futures were selling short—selling contracts at today's price, anticipating they could cover their sales with contracts they bought cheaper tomorrow, next week, or the week after; the lower the price they paid later, the bigger their profit, but if the price went up they would lose.

The commodity Weekly Review of CBWL-Hayden, Stone, Inc., a large New York brokerage house (now simply Hayden Stone, Inc.), said in mid-June, "The new wheat crop situation seems to be shaping up as bearish for both the world and the U.S. markets."

By "bearish" it meant big crops, unexceptional demand, and low prices.

At the end of June the Weekly Review mentioned the "possibility" of "significant" wheat sales to the Soviet Union and said, "While we certainly do not look for a raging bull market, purchases at the current levels ($1.40 to $1.42 for July wheat) could prove to be modestly profitable."

Since the market moves to a large extent on the basis of information (weather forecasts, crop reports, export orders, and the like), industry and speculative traders depend heavily on news sources. A major source is *Milling & Baking News*. Published each Tuesday in Kansas City, Missouri, this slickpaper magazine, averaging about seventy-six pages an issue, has little more than 5,000 subscribers; yet it is the most influential journal in the industry. In addition to its weekly news, it keeps its advertisers advised of day-to-day developments with a daily "Market Quotations" card giving not only market prices but also spot news pertinent to the trade.

On Monday, July 3, the card reported the presence of a Soviet trade delegation in Washington. On Thursday, July 6, it said there were strong indications of Russian grain buying. "Attention centered on whether wheat was included in grain transactions with the Soviet Union," the card said. "Strong indications were that sizeable feed grain business was accomplished by private trade and action in futures indicated some wheat may have been sold."

Who could have dreamed that Continental Grain just the day before had sold the Soviet Union 147 million bushels, 4 million tons, of American wheat?

December futures did rise 4 to 6 cents in Chicago

that first week of July, but Continental was making guarded moves. Michel Fribourg was not revealing his strategy.

Futures would soon be jumping in cattle, hogs, frozen pork bellies (used for bacon), soybean meal, sugar, potatoes, corn, and wheat as supplies of those commodities tightened in 1972. Wheat prices would top $2.70 a bushel before the year was out, the highest they had been since the late 1940s, when American relief agencies sought to avert world famine in the wake of World War II.

But in July, 1972, wheat was a drug on the market.

On Thursday, July 6, Bunge Corporation's vice-president for trading, Carl C. Brasmer, called on the Russians at their New York Hilton suite. He drew a blank. A delegation from the French-owned Louis Dreyfus Corporation was given a better reception the following day, but no deals were made.

By now the U.S. agricultural attaché in Moscow had advised Washington that after spring planting Russia would have a 10 million ton wheat deficit. In fact, the memo from G. Stanley Brown, received at the USDA on July 5, contained a footnote referring to previous memos dating back to February and continuing through spring planting. The memo was made classified information on July 6 and was filed away in the bureaucratic records. Had it been publicized, Moscow's need for foreign wheat would have reverberated through the trade, prices would have gone up before the Exportkhleb officials could buy, and it would have been harder to maintain the $1.63 target price at Gulf ports.

Later it was charged that Central Intelligence Agency operatives had not been able to determine the Soviet crop situation. Although provincial newspapers gave some clues, as did earth-circling satellites, movements of Americans in the Soviet Union were severely limited, and no satellite is sophisticated enough to see what crop is growing where or what condition it is in at any given time. The C.I.A.'s failure to alert Washington to the Soviet crop shortfall was compared with the Agency's fiascos in the 1960 U-2 incident and the 1961 Bay of Pigs. It was said that even the Russians' own Agriculture Ministry was in doubt; the U.S.S.R., explained experts, has no crop reporting system comparable to the one developed in the United States over the past century, and not even the U.S. system can tell from one week to another exactly what effect the weather is having on crops in Kansas, Nebraska, Texas, or the Dakotas.

But its system of state and collective farms may enable Moscow to keep even closer tabs on Soviet crops than Washington does on America's. Somehow the Russians knew by late June that they would want U.S. wheat, which suggests that the Department of Agriculture was remiss in ignoring indications from its Moscow agents and in not knowing earlier what the Russians were up to.

In July, 1972, even after the Soviet agents had secretly concluded almost half their U.S. wheat purchases, Agriculture Secretary Butz was talking corn. Corn, he said, was what the Russians were most likely after.

"They have plenty of wheat for now . . ."

They did not. But along with the wheat they were acquiring elsewhere, the Russians were on their way to buying nearly 12 million tons from the United States—close to two-thirds of all the wheat America normally exports in any one year.

Barney Saunders, a tall, dark, bespectacled Harvard man of about fifty, sat in his office in the Minneapolis suburb of Wayzata and wondered what had become of the Russians. If they were not at the Madison in Washington, where the hell were they?

His suspense ended on Monday morning, July 10. Leonid Kalitenko telephoned to say that the Exportkhleb group was at the New York Hilton. He asked that Cargill send a negotiating team as quickly as possible.

Approaching New York in the company's $2 million Lockheed Jetstar that afternoon, Saunders and his men saw a strange light fall over the city; a partial eclipse was obscuring the sun. When they reached the Hilton at 4:30, prepared to sell corn, they were greeted with another phenomenon. Kalitenko handed Saunders a sheet of hotel stationery and asked him to figure out a sales price, not for corn but for hard red winter wheat.

Before he could make an offer, Saunders, like Fribourg, had to know whether the USDA intended to maintain the $60 a ton target price. Melvin H. Middents, the Cargill wheat specialist, did not visit Carroll Brunthaver in Washington, as Bernard Steinweg had done; but he did telephone. If Brunthaver was shook up by a second inquiry about a possible big Russian wheat purchase, he betrayed no anxiety. The Department of Agriculture, he assured Middents, would guarantee export "equalization" payments, or subsidies.

Even before Saunders and Middents showed up that day, Belousov had been busy. First there had been the phone call from Memphis. On the line was Edward W. ("Ned") Cook, the tall, fiftyish president of Cook Industries in Memphis.

"As you know, Mr. Belousov," Cook drawled, "we're in the grain business. You talked to one of our people ten days ago in Washington. Now I'd like to come up there and see you myself."

"Fine," said Belousov. "When can you be here?"

"I can be at your hotel at 9:30 in the morning."

"Good. I'll see you then."

After that there had been the visit from the Louis Dreyfus people. Dreyfus, a French-controlled firm, shares with Cook Industries some 20 percent of all international grain trade, although it would be hard to say which firm has the bigger share. Philip H. McCaull, Dreyfus' executive vice-president, had first learned of the Russians' presence in New York on Wednesday, July 5, and met with them two days later. Nikolai Belousov asked him at that meeting to make an offer on wheat the following week.

Dreyfus made its offer on Monday, July 10, and after some hours of negotiating the Russians concluded an agreement to buy 750,000 tons from Louis Dreyfus.

At 5:00 the next morning, the Cook Industries Lockheed Jetstar, a luxurious twin to the Cargill plane, left Memphis International Airport with Ned Cook, his grain division director Willard Sparks, a pilot, and a copilot. They touched down at LaGuardia at 8:30, phoned the Hilton, and were told the Russians could not see them until 4:30 that afternoon.

While Cook and Sparks cooled their heels, the Exportkhleb officials met with Michel Fribourg and his Continental traders. In finalizing the July 5 contract for 4 million tons of wheat, Belousov upped the figure to over 5 million tons.

Continental's contracts called for payment in U.S. dollars, to be paid in cash against shipping documents as the grain moved out of U.S. ports. The sales were not contingent on the U.S.S.R.'s obtaining credit, but even the preliminary contracts initialed July 5 contained provision, at the Russians' request, for documentation and other mechanics of payment to be changed in the event the Russians did obtain financing. This was Continental's first intimation that the Soviets might be negotiating for a line of credit from the Commodity Credit Corporation.

After the Continental people had left, it was Cargill's turn. Virtually at the same time that Bobby Fischer (black) and Boris Spassky (white) finally sat down to play chess in Reykjavik, the Russians in New York were making another move. Nikolai Belousov agreed to buy a million tons of hard red winter wheat from Cargill.

"It was the biggest order I ever had in my life," Barney Saunders said later. He had heard reports that Continental was booking unusually large tonnages of ocean shipping for transit to Soviet ports, but how was he to know that Michel Fribourg had sold the Russians nearly 10 million tons of grain, including 5 millions tons of wheat?

As Saunders, Mel Middents, and Tom Connally, the head of Cargill's New York office, came out of a Hilton elevator at 4:30, they were greeted by Ned Cook, who was about to go up to the Exportkhleb suite.

"Hey," said Cook. "You fellows been up to what I'm getting ready to do?"

The Cargill men just grinned. They were to meet the Russians for dinner at the posh Four Seasons Restaurant in the Seagram Building on Park Avenue, but they did not mention it.

By the time Cook and Sparks arrived at Suite 4201 for their appointment, the Russians were tired. They had put in a hard day. But they soon settled down to business. Cook had expected to sell corn, but he was prepared with wheat prices. Unlike the others, he had not checked with Carroll Brunthaver about the export subsidy, but when Belousov, after some haggling over price, agreed to buy 300,000 tons of hard red winter wheat, Cook made the deal.

To celebrate, he broke out a bottle of his personal bourbon, Cook's Cotton Special, 107 proof. The Russians liked it. And before the meeting broke up at 7:00, the Russians had accepted Ned Cook's invitation to visit Memphis.

In the week that followed, when the Democrats in Miami Beach nominated South Dakota Senator George McGovern as their presidential candidate and Missouri Senator Thomas Eagleton as McGovern's hand-picked running mate, the Russians were in Canada, exercising an option arranged earlier in the year to buy a million tons of Canadian wheat.

On Tuesday, July 18, the day they returned to hot, muggy New York, Clifford Pulvermacher was in town talking to Walter C. Klein, president of Bunge Corporation, who offered him a job as manager of Bunge's Washington office.

Ned Cook that day flew in his Jetstar to New York to keep a date with Belousov, Kalitenko, and Sakun. He had arranged for them to be driven to LaGuardia Airport, and by early evening he had set them down in Memphis.

The arrival was cloaked in secrecy and the visitors were quickly whisked off to the Memphis Country Club, where Cook had arranged suites for his guests. At 7:30 cocktails were served, with cheese puffs and bacon-wrapped chestnuts as hors d'oeuvres. Dinner began with crab meat mimosa, followed by tournedos Rossini, broccoli hollandaise, and a salad of Bibb lettuce with watercress and bacon. For dessert there were brandied macaroons with coffee chip ice cream topped with nuts and a cherry.

In Reykjavik, Boris Spassky blundered and lost; after five games he was tied with Fischer and would never lead again. At Port Said, Russian troops were being removed from Egypt "by mutual consent" of Moscow and Cairo. But in Memphis the Russians were in full command, laughing as they teased their "capitalist" hosts, mischievously evading questions about their plans.

The next morning, Ned Cook picked up the Russians and took them to his offices where another wheat order was discussed. But the visitors were tired of talking business. They asked to see a department store. At Goldsmith's, in Southland Mall, they bought gifts for their wives and children.

When his guests asked to see the Mississippi, Cook phoned a friend who owned a fifty-eight-foot Chris-Craft cabin cruiser and took the party out on the river for the afternoon. It was not an idle afternoon; unbusinesslike as they looked in their summer sport shirts, Belousov and Cook signed a contract for another 300,000 tons of hard red winter wheat for export to the Soviet Union.

By then the Russians had had enough of fancy restaurants, so dinner was an outdoor barbecue at the home of Willard Sparks. The visitors helped with the steak-broiling.

The next day, Thursday, July 20, the Russians returned to New York, but not before taking a motor tour of Memphis. And Ned Cook did not just show them "the part of town where people live in $100,000 houses." Kalitenko remarked about the large number of single family houses.

Back in New York, the men from Exportkhleb received a visit from Cargill's Barney Saunders, who had known them for about nine years and was making a social call. "The nature of my visit was as much personal as customer relations," he said later. "No buying or selling was discussed, but the impression I got from our meeting was that the Russians had completed their buying."

On Friday, July 21, Belousov and company left New York for Moscow, via Amsterdam. They had bought all the wheat and feed grains they had come for, but thus far only they knew how much they had bought.

5.

Four days earlier, the editor of *The Southwestern Miller* in Kansas City had received a mysterious telephone call.

The trade paper, now called *Milling & Baking News,* has been headed since 1967 by Morton I. Sosland, an energetic Harvard man in his late forties whose family founded the journal half a century ago and has owned it ever since. Sosland has many other interests, including primitive art; his private collection is one of the best in the world.

As editor of the key publishing enterprise in the milling and baking industry, Sosland is in a unique position to influence the futures markets; it is a responsibility he does not take lightly. So Sosland was understandably suspicious about the telephone call he received on July 17.

The call was from London. The caller—Sosland did not catch the name—said he was an editor of *The Financial Times,* he spoke with an English accent, and Sosland had no immediate reason to doubt him. He had high regard for *The Financial Times.*

"We are running a story," said the man, "about cer-

tain purchases of American wheat by the Soviet Union.
I would like to check some of our facts. I would also like
your impression of how the American public will react
to these sales."

Sosland remembers saying cheerily, "Fire away." But
he was quite unprepared for the caller's news.

"You know," the man said, "our paper has very fine
intelligence sources behind the Iron Curtain. We have
learned through an indiscretion on the part of a Russian
official that the Soviets have bought 5 million tons each
of wheat, corn, and barley from the United States. We
are going to publish a story to that effect. Do these figures
agree with yours?"

Sosland, who had been standing at his desk, sat down
hard. Five million tons?

On July 13, he had sent out the daily Market Quotations card with a notation that "Heavy futures activity
and ship chartering again confirm mammoth, but as yet
unconfirmed, sales of wheat and other grains to USSR. No
consensus was yet apparent on indicated sales total or
breakdown, but many felt that size would be 'unprecedented.'"

On July 14, the card had said, "Trade estimates of
Soviet purchases were mostly around 100 million bushels,
near 2,750,000 metric tons, wheat." That amount would
indeed be "unprecedented."

Still, the price of December wheat futures hovered
about the $1.56 level, up from the lows of May and June,
but no higher than at times in March and April. Trading
floors buzzed with rumors, but there were always rumors.

"How much of that Russian business can you believe?" one trader asked. "All I know is, we're getting a
bumper crop. It's always a matter of supply and demand,
and this year there's certainly no lack of supply. I'm selling futures, not buying."

Sosland had spoken to many key figures in the grain trade the previous week. Nobody had suggested that the Russians might buy even three million tons, much less five. It was a staggering total, really unthinkable.

He paused, and said, "I can't believe it."

But the caller made it evident he was no amateur. He asked, for example, whether Sosland thought the USDA would act to hold down prices by selling freely from its Commodity Credit Corporation (CCC) reserves.

"I would think so," Sosland replied. "Remember, it's an election year. High wheat prices could put pressure on the President's Price Commission to allow an increase in bread prices; Mr. Nixon will no doubt do all he can to avoid the embarrassment of newspaper headlines blaming high bread prices on Soviet wheat sales."

"I disagree," said the caller. "Look how the administration is defending high beef prices. Your Mr. Nixon is obviously out to win the farm vote; he won't be too upset about a penny rise in the price of bread."

Curious. The more the man talked—and the conversation went on for half an hour—the more sophisticated he appeared. Sosland had rarely encountered such savvy about U.S. politics even among American grain experts.

"I thought his figures were wild," Sosland remembers, "but he was clearly no babe in the woods. At the end of our talk I asked him again, 'Are you sure about those figures? Five million tons of wheat? Five million of corn?' He was positive."

December wheat futures on July 17 were at about $1.62 a bushel, a new high for the year but well below prices in some previous years. Sosland knew that the export figures he had been given, if true, could make the market take a leap. Was somebody trying to use him to push prices up?

Sosland called in staff members responsible for market reports. They were as incredulous as he about the figures from London.

Melvin Sjerven, senior editor, Markets, suggested they test the information on executives of grain companies likely to have been involved in any sales to the Soviets. Phone calls went out to Continental, to Cargill, and to other big grain trading firms. The reaction was uniformly one of amazement; Sosland was cautioned in no uncertain terms against publishing the figures he had received.

"If we had printed inaccurate reports," Sosland says, "we would have destroyed our reputation for credibility." But on July 18, the day after the phone call from London, *The Southwestern Miller* came out with a guarded "guess" that the Soviets might possibly have purchased 100 million bushels of U.S. wheat, a bit over half the 5 million tons claimed by the mystery voice on the overseas phone.

Again and again in that third week of July, Sosland received phone calls from his informant in London. On the second or third call he asked the man to repeat his name. It was "John Smith."

"In all honesty and innocence," Sosland says, "I don't remember even smiling and wondering. I had my operator call *The Financial Times* in London; she reported the paper did have a Smith on its staff. And the story did appear in *The Financial Times,* citing the 5 million ton figures."

The London story got no pickup in the American press. Prices for December wheat futures remained at levels between $1.59 and $1.64 a bushel.

Smith called four or five times that week, twice in a single day. He just wanted to visit and "to express confidence in his information about the quantities of wheat and feed grains the Russians had bought." Often the chats went on for some time. Sosland wondered if perhaps *The Financial Times* had an international WATS line, but although firms such as Continental Grain maintain leased wires to points overseas, international WATS lines as such do not exist. Smith always called station to station, direct dial; the rate for such calls from London to Kansas City was $5.40 for the first three minutes, $1.80 for each additional minute, plus tax. The man in London was running up an extravagant phone bill.

His calls continued for nearly a month. During the week of July 24, Smith told of severe setbacks in the Russian spring wheat crop. Soviet authorities, he said, were anxious to avoid publicity lest prices go up; they were also concerned lest the Western press blame Soviet crop failures on the Communist system.

By now December wheat futures had climbed to about $1.75 a bushel, though they soon fell back by more than a dime. Smith, according to Sosland, "had an impressive command of the intricacies of futures contracts, delivery intentions, cash premiums, and other technical matters. He seemed genuinely interested in the squeeze on American bakers and inquired about efforts they might be making to obtain price relief as the wheat market steadily advanced and their costs kept climbing.

"It was in that week of July 24 that he first predicted all U.S. wheat futures would rise above $2 a bushel. I could only gasp."

Smith revealed things only insiders could have known. He told of an early meeting between the Russians and an important trading company. A top official of the company said to Belousov, "We have a feeling you have bought wheat from other people. We do not want to trade with you unless you tell us how much hard winter wheat you have already bought." One of the Russians showed the company officials the door. When Sosland asked the company's president about the incident later, he confirmed it, and was amazed that Sosland could have known.

Sosland was beginning to wonder. Was Smith really a reporter, or an editor? Even for a staff man on one of the world's most prestigious financial newspapers, the man seemed to know too much. Smith's calls often came within an hour of the U.S. market close, 1:15 Kansas City time, midevening London time. On July 31 he called at an unusual hour, 8:30 A.M. Kansas City time. All out of breath, and saying he had no time to talk, he asked the operator to leave a message for the editor. Morton Sosland, speaking on another line, did a double take when he saw the message his secretary handed him:

"Mr. Smith called to say the Russian buying mission has returned to New York to purchase more grain."

More? Sosland phoned some export firms. Yes, they had only just learned the news themselves. (Some had not yet heard.) After barely a week's absence, the Soviet buyers were back in New York. Mr. Smith, or whoever he was, had proved himself an extraordinary source of information. Within the day, Sosland heard his familiar crisp English voice on the phone once again.

"I have learned, Mr. Sosland, that the Soviet gentlemen had purchased more than 5 million tons of wheat even before they went back to Moscow. Now they will buy considerably more. The total wheat purchase will be close to 7½ million tons."

The Russians had, in fact, bought close to that amount on their first visit.

It was sweltering in Moscow when the Belousov party arrived home. Temperatures climbed into the mid-90s, with high humidity. Muscovites, unaccustomed to such heat or to humidity above 30 percent, were suffering. There was little or no air-conditioning.

UN Secretary General Kurt Waldheim was just ending a visit to the city. He was full of praise for Soviet efforts to ease relations with the United States, and full of concern about U.S. bombing of dikes in North Vietnam.

East of the capital in Shatura, famous as the site of the first electric power plant built by the Bolsheviks after the Revolution, normally soggy peat bogs were afire, ignited by burning peat moss set ablaze by careless fishermen, tourists, or illegal hunters. The peat ran twenty to thirty feet deep and the fire, traveling underground, often surfaced twenty yards from where it supposedly had been extinguished. Forests and peat bogs were also burning in Yegorevsk, in Pavlopossadsk, in Noginsk, and more distantly in the regions of Kalinin, Vladimir, and Katrova. Smoke from the nearby fires was polluting the Moscow air. A thick blue shroud hung over the hot city, making eyes water. Visibility was cut to 200 yards; people with sinus trouble were especially miserable.

Much worse for the Russians, the news from the *kolkhozy* (collective farms) and the *sovkhozy* (state farms) was almost uniformly bad. Except for the Asian steppes of Kazakhstan, the virgin lands first plowed by Nikita Khrushchev in 1953, Soviet farms had received little rain. Dry winds were blowing the fields to dust, the wheat was wilting.

Belousov, Kalitenko, and Sakun were not displeased to learn they had been ordered back to America for more wheat.

On Monday morning, July 31, while Smith in London was telephoning so breathlessly to Kansas City, Leonid

Kalitenko at the New York Hilton was calling Barney Saunders in Wayzata and Ned Cook in Memphis.

Would Mr. Saunders please come to New York.

Would Mr. Cook please come to New York.

"By this time," Saunders said later, "rumors of the size of Russian wheat demand were growing. On the basis of published USDA figures on wheat production, carry-over, domestic consumption, and exports, Cargill had prepared a study of an apparent maximum of hard red winter wheat available for 'extraordinary demand' such as Russian exports. Our analysis had been completed by July 27 or 28. Whitney MacMillan, Mel Middents, and I took this analysis with us to meet with the Russians in New York."

But when they asked Belousov that afternoon for a commitment on the maximum amount of hard red winter wheat the Russians would buy from the United States, the Exportkhleb chief refused to give any guarantee. The talks went on into the evening, but ended without a sale.

Ned Cook arrived the next morning and reached an agreement with the Russians to sell them another 300,000 tons of hard red winter wheat. That brought the total Cook & Company Soviet wheat sales to 900,000 tons.

Later in the day Belousov bought another 1.5 million tons of winter wheat from Phil McCaull of the Louis Dreyfus firm.

And before the day was over, the Cargill group, having put together an offer, made its second sale; the Russians agreed to buy another million tons of hard red winter wheat. And to have dinner with Barney Saunders and his associates at the chic L'Aiglon Restaurant on Manhattan's East Fifty-fifth Street.

In Reykjavik that day, Fischer and Spassky had ended their ninth game in a draw; Fischer led 5½ games to 3½. In London, the price of free gold hit a new high of $70 an ounce. In Washington, the Food and Drug Administration anounced a ban on the use of the hormone diethylstilbestrol (DES) in livestock feed, a move that was expected to increase beef prices by $3\frac{1}{2}$ cents a pound. Clifford Pulvermacher reported for work that day at his new job with Bunge Corporation. In Moscow, Commerce Secretary Peter G. Peterson announced that his talks at the Kremlin on expanded East-West trade had ended in a deadlock; newspapermen inferred that the Vietnam War issue had blocked agreement; Peterson left for Warsaw. In Chicago, December wheat futures advanced $1\frac{7}{8}$ to $1.64\frac{7}{8}$; the cash price of wheat was $1.58.

And in New York in just one day the shrewd buyers of Exportkhleb had acquired for the people of the Soviet Union more wheat than Americans eat in two months.

Wheat by now was no longer in a buyers' market. In addition to the 3.5 million tons they had contracted earlier to buy from Canada, the Russians had bought another 1.5 million tons of Canadian wheat. France and Argentina had no more wheat to sell. Australia could sell only a million tons, Sweden half a million. The United States no longer had any competition.

No other country in the world was in a position to export substantial quantities of wheat.

But although it was now well aware—both jubilantly and painfully—that the Russians had bought more than a sixth of the U.S. wheat crop, the USDA was still paying an export subsidy on every bushel the Russians were buying. In early July the subsidy had been only a few cents a bushel. As prices rose, so did the subsidy. It inched up to between 10 and 15 cents. And on August 3 it jumped to 24 cents.

For on that day the wheat market went wild. In his

August 2 issue of *The Southwestern Miller,* Morton Sosland reported that purchases of U.S. wheat by the U.S.S.R. had totaled about 7 million metric tons. There were indications, the breadstuffs newsmagazine reported, that additional purchases were being made.

Indeed they were. Having bought nearly 3 million tons of wheat the day before, Belousov and his comrades on August 2 bought another 950,000 tons—600,000 from Bunge and 350,000 from the Swiss-controlled Garnac Grain Company. Total Soviet purchases were now over 11 million tons, one fourth of the U.S. wheat crop.

A major news source in the grain market is the Reuters News Service, whose Washington commodity reporter is Reginald Watts. Toward the end of July, Reuters claimed some months later, it too had received calls from Sosland's John Smith, who was told that Watts was on leave. Smith, according to Reuters staff people, said he was one of Watts' sources.

"The Russians," he told them, "have bought at least 25 million tons of U.S. wheat. I'm tipping you off so you can scoop the other wire services."

Urging them to waste no time, Smith left a New York phone number where he could be reached.

Reuters called Watts at home, according to the story. Watts called the number that Smith had left and found himself talking to a Puerto Rican woman in the Bronx. Wrong number? Or had Smith left a false number?

Meanwhile Smith allegedly called Reuters again. Had they sent out the story on their wire?

"Reggie Watts will be flaming mad if you don't," he warned a Reuters editor. And he left another phone number.

Again the bureau called Watts at home. Again Watts tried to reach Smith. And again he was connected with someone in the Bronx, this time a different someone, but still not anyone who knew beans about wheat. Watts says he forgot about Smith until two months later, when Sosland broke the story about his mysterious caller.

On August 3, Watts sent out this story on the Reuters wire:

"Russian trade delegates, currently in New York, are placing buying orders for further substantial quantities of U.S. wheat and feed grains, according to informed sources here.

"The unexpected return visit of the Soviet officials earlier this week remains shrouded in secrecy, but discussions are known to have taken place with at least two big grain export houses in New York."

Now at last the market began to believe. The Russians obviously had bought a lot more wheat than anyone had thought. Responding vigorously to this realization, wheat futures moved up sharply. So did the cash price of wheat. And the subsidy moved up right along with it, although not enough yet to make the USDA nervous.

Continental, Cargill, Dreyfus, Cook, and the others were nervous enough. Each had sold wheat it did not own. Each was engaged in the delicate process of trying to acquire wheat without disturbing the precarious price balance of the market. No company knew how much wheat any other company had sold the Russians; none knew the total amount of the Soviet purchase.

Continental had, in fact, sold at least 5.5 million tons, Dreyfus 2.25 million, Cargill 2 million, Cook 900,000, Bunge 600,000, and Garnac 550,000. The figures are understated; they total 11.7 million tons, about 430 million bushels. Exportkhleb more probably bought 440 million bushels, nearly 12 million tons. It was a staggering amount, but the total was still a Russian secret.

Even knowing only its own commitment, an export firm needed cool nerves to sign such large contracts. Traders would have to play a cautious game, avoiding obvious moves that would drive up prices as they quietly made their purchases and assembled their stores.

But somebody seemed to be trying to blow the cover of secrecy off the sales.

On Friday, August 4, Mr. Smith called Morton Sosland from London to say the Russians had bought an additional 5,250,000 tons of wheat to make their total U.S. wheat purchase 13.25 million tons. (He had allegedly given Reuters a figure nearly twice that amount, but many in the trade are inclined to doubt the Reuters story.)

The Financial Times, Smith said, was going to use the 13.25 million ton figure; he was giving it to Sosland ahead of publication "to let you have a scoop."

Although they still knew only their own company sales, exporters were now less skeptical of the big figures Sosland tested on them. On the basis of what he learned from them, Sosland stated in his August 9 Market Quotations card that the Soviets had bought 250 million bushels of U.S. wheat, and that there were strong indications that another 150 million bushels had been contracted for. This would make a total of 400 million bushels, or almost 11 million metric tons.

Smith phoned to tell Sosland he was still being too conservative.

"They are buying 14 million tons, sir, not eleven. And 10 million tons of corn. I might be wrong, but by no more than 250,000 tons. They are selling gold to pay for the grain."

This time Smith's grain figures were way too high. But the Russians were buying something else. After agreeing to a third purchase of 300,000 tons of wheat from Ned Cook on August 1, Belousov had asked Cook to return on Friday the 4 to sell feed grains. And when Cook arrived for breakfast that morning he was asked to offer soybeans.

Soybean meal makes an ideal high-protein feed for livestock. So does fishmeal from Peruvian anchovies. (Some U.S. firms, including Cargill, Inc., are active in processing Peru's anchovies.) But in June, 1972, the Peruvian anchovy catch "had fallen to only about 10 percent of normal." The quotation is from a C.I.A. report, a long-classified intelligence report prepared in October by the C.I.A.'s Office of Economic Research. Some experts had blamed the low anchovy catch on overfishing, but the C.I.A. attributed it to a "mysterious" warm current Peruvians call "El Niño de Navedad," the Christmas Child.

Anchovies thrive in the cool, north-moving Humboldt Current, but every December the Christmas Child moves south to northern Peru, only to be pushed away in March by the Humboldt Current. Every seven years the warm current for some reason moves far south of its normal range, driving the anchovies beyond the reach of Peruvian fishing fleets. In 1972, the Humboldt Current was peculiarly weak and "El Niño" persisted much longer than usual. Since processing anchovies into fishmeal is Peru's leading manufacturing activity and supplies nearly a third of her foreign earnings, the disappearance of the anchovies struck a severe blow to Peru's economy. It also raised the price of fishmeal on the world market.

And it boosted demand—and prices—for soybeans and soybean meal, which farmers could use instead of fishmeal in livestock feed.

Russia does not have the climatic conditions needed to grow soybeans. America's Corn Belt has ideal conditions: a long summer with a lot of rain at the start, a hot spell, and a lot of rain at the end. Insignificant in the 1930s, the U.S. soybean crop is now second only to corn in value and is the nation's top agricultural export in dollar earnings. The United States grows about 1.2 billion bushels of soybeans a year (32.5 million tons).* This is 72 percent of the world crop (China grows 15 percent); 94 percent of the soybeans in world trade come from the United States, which in 1969–70 exported nearly 40 percent of its crop. (No export subsidy is paid; since U.S. soybeans have almost no competition, no export subsidy is needed.)

Knowing that the Soviets wanted to increase their livestock production, other grain companies had tried to sell Exportkhleb soybeans; only Cook was able to pull it off. At breakfast with the Russians on August 4, the Tennessean reached a verbal agreement to sell them a million tons of soybeans.

Cook was less chummy with the Russians than some other traders were; industry sources wondered how he had made the deal in soybeans, and there was talk that he had promised to help them install crushing plants and give them technical expertise. Cook says this is "completely untrue.

"We made no promises of any kind or nature whatsoever, except I did say, 'I'm going to come over there every three months, or meet you somewhere, to be damn sure we're performing the way we ought to perform. And I want you to tell me flat out if we're doing anything that's not according to the contract or is not the most expeditious way to get this business handled.' " (Cook more than made good on his vow; he visited Moscow in September, 1972, and again in November, a week before Barney Saunders

---

* Like wheat, soybeans measure about 36.74 bushels to the metric ton. Corn and rye measure about 39.37 bushels, barley 45.93, and oats 68.89.

of Cargill was there; he saw the Russians in Paris in January, 1973, in New York a few weeks later, and periodically thereafter.)

By Friday afternoon the men from Exportkhleb were tired. The expansive Ned Cook suggested a working holiday. While John Smith in London was phoning Morton Sosland in Kansas City, Cook was flying the Russians south to Florida in his Jetstar. At his four-bedroom house at Lost Tree Village, near Palm Beach, Cook entertained with his W. C. Fields imitations. When Leonid Kalitenko said he was a Perry Como fan, Cook dug up an old Como record; Kalitenko reciprocated with Russian folk songs delivered in a charming tenor voice.

In Chicago that day, wheat futures were hitting new life-of-contract highs. So were soybean futures, up the 10 cent-limit as word reached traders that a deal had been made with the Russians. Soybeans were the topic of conversation at Lost Tree Village. As Americans talked about Sargent Shriver, the running mate George McGovern had picked that day to replace Tom Eagleton, the men from Moscow were discussing their soybean contract, which they jokingly called "SB 001," a reference to the "007" code name Ian Fleming pinned on his James Bond.

On Saturday, between swims in ocean and pool, the Russians signed the 300,000 ton wheat contract they had agreed to four days earlier. And they signed a contract to buy a million tons of soybeans.

Number 1 yellow soybeans had closed in Chicago the day before at $3.61½ a bushel, up more than a nickel from the day before; by the end of the year they would top $4.10 a bushel and then climb to $7.00 (they retreated when Peru resumed her anchovy fishing in March of 1973 but jumped to well over $8.00 a bushel in May when the Peruvian anchovy catch proved disappointing). Cook will not say what price he got, but his sale must have been in the neighborhood of $130 million.

With business done, the Russian trio was ready for fun and they had no Ninotchka to scold them. From Saturday through Monday, Ned Cook showed them the sights of southern Florida. At Lion Country Safari, they were driven through a park where giraffes, lions, elephants, and zebras roam about uncaged. But at a small coffee shop in Miami Beach they encountered the real America.

"I would like a homburger," Belousov told the counter girl.

"Just wait your turn, buddy," she answered.

"I said I would like a homburger."

"And I said keep your shirt on. I'll get to you when I have time."

Ned Cook, who relates the story with a chuckle, flew his guests back to New York on Tuesday, August 8. He would not see them again until September, in Moscow.

By August 8, Morton Sosland knew his Mr. Smith was not on the staff of *The Financial Times*. He had phoned the London paper and found that although it did have a Mr. Smith, his first name was not John and he was a literary editor, not a commodities expert. The paper's agricultural staff could not recall the source of the 5-million ton Soviet wheat and corn purchase figures it had reported in July. Staff members did say they had received telephone tips from a man who called himself Veovosky; he claimed he was an East German interested in Soviet grain buying activity.

Sosland's phone call to London turned up another curiosity: on August 8, the day he learned from Sosland that *The Southwestern Miller* planned to publish a 400 million bushel figure (and insisted it was too low), Mr.

Smith (or Herr Veovosky) phoned *The Financial Times,* and reported the figure the Kansas City paper was going to publish.

When the mystery voice called that day from London, Sosland let Mr. Smith know that he was well aware Smith was not with *The Financial Times.*

"He was not the least bit perturbed," Sosland recalls. "He said he was part of 'a secret information office' with headquarters in London. What could we say? We had learned previously that secret 'James Bondish' organizations did exist in London, extra-governmental groups that were expert in all kinds of intelligence. I told the man that one of the world's leading grain trading companies was so impressed with his knowledge that they were interested in becoming his client. Funny. Here was this tremendous company, quite prepared to pay handsome fees, and the London man airily dismissed it. He said, 'Oh, we don't need that kind of client.' "

When Sosland asked for a number where he could reach Smith in London, suggesting that *The Southwestern Miller* bear some of the phone bill expense, the offer was laughingly rejected.

"Say, by the way," Smith remarked casually, "you know the Russians aren't in New York this afternoon."

"No? Where are they?"

"They're in Wayzata."

When Smith rang off, Sosland phoned a friend at Cargill.

"I understand you have some visitors there today."

There was a long pause. The Cargill man finally said, "What do you mean?"

"I mean the Russians are there, aren't they?"

Shortly after stepping off Ned Cook's Jetstar in New York that morning, Belousov, Kalitenko, and Sakun had stepped right on Cargill's Jetstar. They had been flown at their own request to Duluth where they inspected a Cargill grain elevator facility. And from Duluth they had been set down at the Minneapolis-St. Paul International Airport for their first visit to Cargill headquarters. No publicity attended their arrival. How could Smith in London have known about it?

To the suggestion that Smith's calls might not have come from London, Sosland replies, "An overseas phone call has a special timbre. I had my operator listen in and she knew from long experience that these were not domestic calls. Actually, we got the impression Smith had been in this country several times during the course of our month-long telephone relationship, but almost all the calls were from London. I suppose they could have come from the Bahamas, but if they weren't from someplace overseas then somebody was going to a great deal of trouble to put us on."

Sosland recalls something else. "Whenever we were having a disagreement on some aspect of the Russian grain buying, he would address me in his British tones not as 'Mr. Sosland' but more often than not as 'Mr. Morton Sosland.' My linguistic expert tells me there is only one people in the world who uses complete names like that in everyday conversation, and that is the Russians."

Smith phoned Sosland twice again, on August 9 and 10, not from London but from Paris.

"I am about to leave on an important trip," he said on the 10th. "I am calling to inquire as to what you may have heard about Chinese wheat purchases. It is my impression that the Chinese Embassy here in Paris will be negotiating for U.S. wheat through Louis Dreyfus and other French companies with U.S. connections. I have heard guesses that the Chinese will need 3 million metric tons for starters, and . . ."

To this day the identity of Sosland's caller remains a mystery. But speculation as to who he was had only begun.

On Wednesday, August 9, *The Financial Times* in London, with Sosland's permission, reported the purchase by Soviet Russia of nearly 11 million tons (400 million bushels) of U.S. wheat. The story ran under a banner headline with *The Southwestern Miller* credited as the source.

In Wayzata that day Nikolai Belousov and Barney Saunders were signing the contract for the sale of a million tons of hard red winter wheat agreed to in New York eight days before. Smith had told Morton Sosland of an early incident in which Belousov had stormed out of a luncheon meeting with Cargill after an angry dispute over the terms of a contract; the fact that Cargill sold Exportkhleb far less grain than did Continental, and even less than the Louis Dreyfus firm, suggests that the story may have some foundation, although Cargill does not confirm it.

Whatever disagreements they may have had in the past, Cargill-Exportkhleb relations were now harmonious. The Russians were in high good humor. They had been entertained the night before at a dinner party in Wayzata at the home of Whitney MacMillan, one of Cargill's executive vice-presidents. They had slept in a suite at the North Star Center across from the Minneapolis Athletic Club.

After signing the contract in Wayzata, the Russians, at their request, were taken to the farm of a soybean grower east of Minneapolis. They romped jovially with the farmer's little boy, tousling his straw-colored hair, carrying him on their shoulders. But they gave careful scrutiny to the equipment used in soybean cultivation, and they asked serious questions.

In Reykjavik that afternoon, Fischer and Spassky ended their twelfth game in a draw; Bobby now led 7 games to 5. In Washington, the USDA finally was beginning to catch on; it announced that Cook Industries in Memphis had sold the Russians a million tons of soybeans valued at "about $100 million"; but it displayed its ignorance about Exportkhleb's grain-buying when it made front-page headlines with the estimate that Moscow's grain buy might total $1 billion over the next twelve months, "about half of it in wheat." In Chicago, December wheat futures closed at $1.82, a dime above the spot price.

Late in the afternoon, Nikolai Belousov, Leonid Kalitenko, and Paul Sakun climbed into the big, roomy Cargill Jetstar and were flown to New York.

They remained in town for another nine days, meeting often with Michel Fribourg and his people to finalize contracts drawn up more than a month before. In most other years Fribourg would have been at Castallaras, on the French Riviera, where Michel and his pretty German-born wife, Mary Ann (née Steinweg), usually summer, or at Crans sur Sierre, the hideaway in the Swiss Alps where they have gone for fifteen years. The Fribourgs spent the summer of 1972 at their Manhattan townhouse. After hard business sessions at Continental's modern offices high up in a downtown skyscraper, Michel sometimes took his visitors home to the European ambience of the charming house on Seventy-third Street with its Louis XV and Louis XVI furniture, its paneled rooms, its vases of freshly cut flowers, its lively beagle. On the walls were works by Chagall, Modigliani, Pascin, Pissaro, and by the devoted Sunday painter Michel Fribourg. The butler kept the keys to the wine cellar, whose 1,500 dusty bottles, many of them 1928 and 1929 vintage, included some burgundies that bore the name Fribourg, vestiges of the days when Uncle René had an interest in the famed Clos Vougeot vineyards.

On the weekend of August 12 the Fribourgs entertained their Russian visitors at their country place in Norwalk, Connecticut. And on Friday, the 18, the Russians left for Moscow. Returning with them were contracts for nearly 4 million tons of U.S. wheat, over and beyond what they had bought in July, plus the "SB 001" contract for a million tons of soybeans. In less than six weeks the Russians had exceeded the $1 billion figure the USDA had projected for a full year's purchases, but still only Exportkhleb knew the full extent of its buying. And nobody appreciated the significance of what the Russians had done. What Americans did not know would not hurt them. Until later.

6.

Hard red winter wheat, the class of wheat usually in surplus in America, was now in short supply. The export companies had tried to sell Belousov and company spring wheat, which is comparable to most of the wheat grown in Russia. The Russians could have bought spring wheat cheaper than winter wheat, but they would have none of it.

What worried the Russians was a fungus parasite, *Claviceps* (meaning "club-headed") *purpura* (meaning "purple.") The short name is ergot. The purple cockspurs of the ergot fungus contain several alkaloid drugs including one called ergotamine. If accidentally baked in the oven with dough, ergotamine is transformed into LSD, the most powerful hallucinogen known to man. In fact, the man who discovered and purified lysergic acid diethylamine in Switzerland in 1943 used as his raw material the ergot fungus that made Belousov, Kalitenko, and Sakun wary of U.S. spring wheat in 1972. They had good reason.

Just 250 years earlier, on the plains of Astrakhan, Russian fortunes had been given a fatal setback by an epidemic of ergotism, the maddening disease produced by the alkaloid drugs in ergot. Czar Peter Romanov, the six-foot-seven giant who in his youth had earned the name Peter the Great by giving Russia access first to the Black Sea and then to the Baltic, was in 1722 marshaling his Cossacks on the Volga delta. His strategy was to sweep down through the Caucasus mountains into the Asian heartland of the Ottoman Empire. While his cavalry was drawing the Sultan's European forces out of the Ukraine and the Balkans, Peter's navy would sweep the Black Sea clean of Turkish ships and capture the Bosphorus and the Dardanelles. Ukrainians and Balkan Slavs would rise against their Ottoman oppressors, and Russia would gain a clear path to the Mediterranean and the West. It would achieve its national destiny as a major world power.

The plan was a bold one, and although Peter did not know it his timing was perfect. For the Turkish Empire had grown decadent. Its grand vizier had seduced Constantinople's ruling set to his impassioned enthusiasm for growing tulips. Flower power would be no match for Peter power.

Except for ergotism, the plan might well have succeeded. But to feed Peter's Cossacks and their mounts, the serfs of the delta came into Astrakhan with cartloads of rye—rye hay and grain for the horses, rye flour to bake bread for the men. And the rye was infected with ergot fungus.

One night in late August, a horse in the camp beside the Caspian Sea went down with the blind staggers. By dawn, a man's agonized shriek was heard; by noon a hundred horses were down; and by evening scores of cavalrymen were screaming and writhing on the ground. In the following days and weeks, thousands of soldiers and serfs were seized with excruciating muscular convulsions, thousands of others had wild hallucinations, some went insane, and about 20,000 in the neighborhood of Astrakhan died of ergotism.

The burnished pride of Russia's military might was reduced to tin soldiers, and although Russian armies attacked Turkey six times in the centuries that followed, the Turks were never again so vulnerable; the Russians never were able to take the Dardanelles.

Usually it is rye that is infected with ergotism, as it was in the Volga delta in 1722, but ergot can infect other grains as well, and in recent years it has been found in U.S. spring wheat. American millers and bakers, and the U.S. Food and Drug Administration, insist that American milling methods render ergot harmless. There has never been an outbreak of ergotism in the United States. But the Russians in 1972, even if they were not familiar with Peter the Great's experience, must have read about the major epidemic of ergotism that swept parts of Russia in 1926–27. A lot of Russians took bad trips in that epidemic. Many died.

Spring wheat? "Nyet," said Nikolai Belousov.

Hard winter wheat was selling briskly in August of 1972 as the big trading companies covertly bought grain to cover their Russian contracts. On August 10, the day Morton Sosland in Kansas City got his final phone call from John Smith in London, the cash price of wheat was down a bit from the week before, but still was above the $1.77 level at which an export subsidy of 14 cents was theoretically required to maintain the $1.63 target price.

All the export sales had been made with the clear understanding that the USDA would maintain that target price. Continental, Cargill, Dreyfus, and the other companies had been assured of export subsidies that would enable them to export U.S. wheat at $1.63 a bushel even if they had to pay considerably more for the wheat in the U.S. market.

But in Washington, the President's economic advisory troika—George P. Shultz, Herbert Stein, and Caspar W. Weinberger—was demanding a stop. So was the American Bakers Association. The export subsidy was amounting to a raid on the U.S. Treasury; and was contributing to the rise in the price that bakers paid for flour.

Many other countries as well as Russia were buying American wheat in 1972; export subsidies on all the wheat averaged about 35 cents a bushel, much less than the 65 cent average in January, 1964, when America had last exported wheat to the Soviet Union, and infinitely less than the $1.36 subsidy that France was paying exporters in early June, 1972. The average subsidy on U.S. wheat sold to Russia was below 30 cents a bushel, but the number of bushels involved was enormous; multiply 30 cents by 440 million bushels, and the cost to U.S. taxpayers was $132 million, plus another $180 million in export subsidies on wheat shipped to other destinations.

(Taxpayers also would be subsidizing the merchant marine to the tune of nearly $10 a ton, 26 cents a bushel, on about 5½ million tons of grain; and although they were saving millions of dollars in reduced farm subsidies, and on storage and interest charges that had consumed so much tax money in the days of vast unsold surpluses, these savings might well have been realized even if no export subsidies had been paid. The Russians simply would have had to pay higher prices.)

On August 24 the export subsidy was up to 38 cents. That was not enough to maintain the $1.63 target price, not with wheat selling at $2.11 a bushel, but now the market was running away. The government was holding

back on subsidy, believing that the subsidy itself was helping to fuel the market advance.

Under fire now from all sides, the USDA decided it
had to do something. On August 24, a USDA official,
Charles W. Pence, phoned the export companies and asked
them to assemble in Washington the following day. At
the conference on Friday, August 25, Carroll Brunthaver
made a little announcement:

"You will have all of next week, gentlemen, to register
any contracts you wrote before August 23 but have not
yet registered. You will receive subsidy on those contracts
at the rate of 47 cents a bushel. But after next week, you
will have to take your chances; the government can no
longer protect the $1.63 a bushel price."

Millions of bushels were registered for export in the
week beginning August 28. And millions of dollars were
guaranteed in subsidy. But starting August 25, even
though wheat prices continued to mount, the subsidy announced each afternoon was lower by a few cents than it
had been the day before. From 38 cents a bushel it went
down to 34, then to 32. By August 31 it was at 30 cents,
by September 21 at 14 cents, and on Friday, September
22, it stopped altogether.

Some of the export companies benefited more than
others from the subsidies. For just as a company may be
"short on wheat" because it has agreed to sell more than
it holds, it may be "short on subsidy" if it buys wheat but
delays applying for export subsidies on that wheat as the
market advances. If a company expects wheat prices, and
therefore wheat subsidies, to go up, it may very well wait
to register the contracts it has sold for export.

Continental, which sold 191 million bushels of wheat
to the U.S.S.R., applied for subsidies on about 70 million
bushels in mid-July, when the subsidy was only between

13 and 15 cents a bushel. It applied for subsidy on another 50 million bushels, says Continental, the second week in August, when the subsidy was from 31 to 36 cents. When Continental applied for subsidy on 71 million bushels in the final week of August, the subsidy was at its all-time high of 47 cents; but by then, says Continental, the company was registering contracts for wheat on which it had paid prices ranging over $2.10 a bushel to cover the sales it had made. Continental insists it lost money on those 71 million bushels.

Although Cargill made money on overall 1972 sales, it alleges it lost on the Soviet contracts. When it sold a million tons of wheat to the Russians on July 11, it owned less than 7 million bushels; it was "short" the other 30 million. But it would not have to ship the wheat for several months; it was not anticipating further sales to Moscow; there was plenty of time, and Cargill was buying wheat in a deliberate, orderly way. By the end of July it was still short 20 million bushels, the company later reported. Cargill sold another million tons in early August, but it did not finish buying wheat to cover its commitments until September 21. So although Cargill had sold to the Russians at $1.62 a bushel, the big Minneapolis company says it was obliged to pay on average over $2.00 a bushel. Even with export subsidies averaging 33.4 cents, and with hedging operations saving nearly 7 cents, Cargill claims it lost nearly a penny on every bushel it sold to the Russians. And it sold them about 73 million bushels. The independent accounting firm of Peat, Marwick, Mitchell confirms the Cargill statement.

Nevertheless, many critics, without impugning the accounting firm, remain unconvinced. Cargill and other companies, they observe, buy grain and sell it for export to a great many countries. They may lose money on one contract and make money on another. Cargill identified certain purchases and sales as being for Russia, but it would be hard for an exporter to prove that a particular lot of grain bought at a particular price was shipped at a loss to Odessa rather than at a profit to Yokohama.

As for one statistic there is no dispute: export subsidies on the Russian wheat cost U.S. taxpayers over $130 million.

Not least among the ironies of Russia's buying hard winter Kansas wheat was that the wheat's ancestors had come to Kansas just a century earlier from fields in Russia itself.

That wheat was Turkey Red, introduced to the Kansas prairie by Mennonite farmers, refugees from the Crimea where they had developed the wheat from a red-colored seed obtained in Turkey.

These Mennonites, originally from Holland, had fled Spanish persecution in the Lowlands in 1568 and settled in Germany, Switzerland, and eastern Russia. They lived in those countries for 200 years, adopting German as their language and practicing their religion, whose canons forbade them to bear arms or engage in war.

After Russia's Catherine the Great annexed the Crimea in 1783 and expelled the Turks, she offered the Mennonites a large grant of land and promised them they would be exempt from military service, would not have to pay taxes for a period of thirty years, and would have the right to their own churches, schools, and language. Thus did the frugal, industrious Mennonites escape conscription in the Crimean War of the 1850s, but Alexander II, although he liberated the serfs, refused to renew Catherine's promises to the Mennonites. With their privileges due to expire in the early 1880s, the sect cast about for a new home.

America at the time was in the grip of a railroad-building fever. Encouraged by government subsidies and land grants, financiers were hiring gangs to lay tracks across the plains and through the western mountains. By the early 1870s the Atchison, Topeka, and Santa Fe Railroad was seeking farmers to fill its vast land grants and produce crops that would generate freight revenues. To lure homesteaders to Kansas, the railroad sent agents to the East and to Europe, where they distributed circulars offering land at cheap prices (the free land available under the Homestead Act was farther from the railroad and therefore less desirable). The Santa Fe agents offered a passenger fare from New York of only $11. Naturally, they described Kansas as the promised land.

About 400 Mennonite families, some 1,900 people, took the bait, especially when the Santa Fe chartered ships to bring them over from Europe free of charge and built temporary barracks to house them until they could build their own houses. The Mennonites paid the Santa Fe $250,000 in gold for 60,000 acres, and they came to settle in Reno, Harvey, Marion, and McPherson counties. In the next few years, another 16,000 Mennonites left the Crimea, more than half coming to Kansas, with the rest going mostly to Nebraska, North Dakota, and Manitoba province in Canada.

Most families brought with them a bushel or so of hand-picked Turkey Red seed wheat.

Kansas until then had never grown so much as 5 million bushels of wheat. Corn was its crop, and its people ate corn bread spread with sorghum molasses. Now all that began to change. From John Deere's factory in Mo-

line, Illinois, built twenty-five years earlier, plows with self-polishing steel faces that could break the hard-baked sod were spewing forth by the thousands. (Deere & Company still sells more farm equipment than any other manufacturer in the United States.) Chicago was on its way to becoming what poet Carl Sandburg later called the "stacker of wheat." Cyrus McCormick had built a factory there the same year Deere built his in Moline, and McCormick was sending out his patented harvesters to reap the grain; one machine did the work of five men. With the wheat grown by the Mennonites, the new machinery was to revolutionize Great Plains agriculture. Farmers were mortgaging their spreads to buy it.

Most of Kansas was still the Wild West. Texas longhorn steers were being driven as far as 600 miles overland up the Chisholm Trail to the Santa Fe railhead at Abilene, where James ("Wild Bill") Hickok was the law. Russia's Grand Duke Alexis, in the company of General Philip Sheridan and Lieutenant Colonel George Custer, and escorted by William F. ("Buffalo Bill") Cody, had just been shooting bison in western Kansas, where they were still plentiful on the prairies.

But while Wyatt Earp, Bat and Jim Masterson, and Doc Holliday were making legends in "wicked" Dodge City the God-fearing Mennonite countrymen of the Grand Duke Alexis were quietly growing wheat in eastern Kansas.

Like the German Mennonites who had settled Pennsylvania Dutch (*Deutsch*) country two centuries earlier, these Russians were good farmers. With their earnest work ethic, they built great solid barns, reared large families, worked long hours, and farmed assiduously. And their wheat grew as it never had in Mother Russia; far better than the wheat that American-born farmers had brought from eastern farms.

The Americans looked askance at their strange "Roosian" neighbors, who never shaved their beards and whose dress, home life, entertainment, and religious services were so starkly simple. But when the sod-busters saw how the Mennonites' wheat resisted rust and drought, a few overcame their xenophobia and bought seed.

America's population was still under 40 million; more than a third of Americans still lived on farms. But the nation was changing.

In 1877, three years after the Mennonites arrived, the U.S. Supreme Court (in *Munn* v. *Illinois,* 94 U.S. 113) sustained an Illinois action that established state supervision of grain elevators; all subsequent regulation of business by government in the United States stemmed from that landmark decision and those made in the later "Granger Cases." But under President Ulysses S. Grant the federal government seemed more intent on lining its own pockets than on policing businessmen. In the Crédit Mobilier scandal of 1873, the construction company that was building the Union Pacific Railroad was found to have bribed Cabinet members and Congressmen. A financial panic that year, arising from inflated currency, unlimited credit, reckless speculation, and overexpansion, ruined the Wall Street railroad financier Jay Cooke. But while many foreigners were pulling their capital out of the United States, a retired London silk merchant, Sir George Grant, was bringing four Aberdeen Angus bulls to his farm in Victoria, Kansas (named after the Queen by sentimental English aristocrats who came to Kansas). Grant's Angus cattle were the first ever seen in America; they began the ascent of that breed as a major source of U.S. beef.

Chilled steel, used in the moldboard of the plow invented by James Oliver in 1869, was used in 1874 for the rollers installed in Minneapolis by Washburn and Pills-

bury to crush wheat into flour. Of more interest to the
Mennonites was the newly patented barbed wire that was
fencing off land from crop-trampling cattle and changing
the face of the prairie.

In the late 1870s nearly 10 million Chinese and 4
million Bengali died of famine, but in Kansas wheat
covered the plains. It was the get-rich-quick crop. A farm
editor in 1874 cautioned, "Don't risk your *all* on wheat.
Raise corn and hogs, oats, barley, hay, flax, potatoes, sheep,
cattle, poultry, bees—anything that is profitable so that if
any . . . calamities befall you as they have thousands of
wheat growers in the west . . . you may have some other
reliance to depend on." Although subsistence farmers did
plant corn, which required much less soil preparation and
made better animal feed, the cash crop was wheat. And
when crop failures in Europe raised U.S. wheat prices in
1879, the Mennonites and their neighbors waxed prosperous.

Eight years of extraordinary rainfall on the Great
Plains ended in 1886, and in the ten-year drought that
ensued, many wheat farmers wished they had followed the
advice of that farm editor. When the Kansas wheat crop
totaled only 18 million bushels in 1895, the Department
of Agriculture sent its famous agronomist Mark Carleton
out to investigate. Carleton reported that the only good
wheat in the state was the Mennonites' Turkey Red. That
caused a sensation. Farmers clamored for the miracle
wheat, which soon completely replaced soft spring wheat
in Kansas.

Its use spread to Montana, Minnesota, and the Dakotas, where it was grown as hard spring wheat, and to
Nebraska, Texas, and Oklahoma, where it was planted in
the fall. Turkey Red created a Green Revolution long

before that term was thought of. It produced good yields on land where wheat had never grown well before. And it increased overall wheat yields threefold and more.

Had it not been for Turkey Red, brought over from the Crimea by Mennonite farmers a century earlier, Kansas and the other big wheat-growing states would not have had the wheat surplus that permitted the Russians to buy at such attractive prices in 1972.

No subsidies were payable to the export companies until the grain was placed on ships and the bills of lading signed. The deadline for most of the subsidies was May 31, 1973.

But although the Russians had made their buys in July and early August, 1972, and about 68 million bushels had gone out on third country vessels by the end of November, not one bushel of Russian-bought grain left any U.S. port on a U.S. or Soviet ship until early December.

The five preceding months had seen a hubbub of activity on the Italian marble trading floor of the Baltic Exchange in the center of London's financial City. Developed from seventeenth-century coffeehouses where shipping people met to negotiate deals, the Exchange got its name in the following century when so much of its business was with nations bordering on the Baltic Sea. Today the Baltic Exchange is the chief marketplace for chartering carriers on all the world's seas.

Deals, or "fixtures," arranged under the Exchange's high-domed ceiling involve most of the 33,500 vessels in the world merchant shipping fleet. Several billion dollars worth of business is done there each year, all of it on a gentlemanly basis that derives from the old coffeehouses.

One man shakes another man's hand and says, "It's

fixed." And the men operate under the code of the Baltic Exchange motto, "Our word is our bond." (A ship-broker firm tried in 1971 to obtain membership for a Miss Margaret Pattle, one of its brokers, but despite a *Times* of London editorial deploring what it called "prep school psychology," the Exchange stood by its rule excluding women from membership.)

It was here that the Russians, in the summer and fall of 1972, were mobilizing much of the shipping they would need to carry all the grain they had bought from the United States, Canada, and other countries. And they were doing it with the same clandestine canniness they had employed to buy American grain.

Derek Prentis, a London shipping agent quoted in *The Wall Street Journal* by Bowen Northrup, says, "They would come out one day and say, 'We might be interested in a bulk carrier.' They would pick it up and tuck it away (hire it). Two or three days later they would come back and pick up another. They covered quite a bit of the market that way."

According to Prentis, the Exchange's camaraderie permits a good exchange of information. "You get shrewd. You get to know a fellow, you get to know his reactions, you can tell if he really is interested in your proposition."

The Exchange is also a good place to withhold information. "If you disclose your market information to all and sundry," says Prentis, "you'll never do business."

One great withholder of information was W. H. Pim Junior & Co., Continental Grain Co.'s London branch. Pim Junior has never disclosed how much tonnage it lined up to ship the grain sold by Continental.

But although the Russians were able to cover substantial amounts of their commitment without raising tonnage rates, the cat got out of the bag in September. A broker for a grain shipper let it be known one day that he had a single consignment of 100,000 tons to ship.

Immediately the rate shot up from $9 a ton to $12, although it subsequently backed off a bit.

But by then the Russians had contracted for most of their shipping. Even before coming to the London market, they had booked ships in Genoa, Paris, Oslo, and other ports.

What delayed shipments on U.S. and Soviet flag vessels was a dispute over freight terms. A maritime agreement signed October 14 had allocated one-third of the cargoes to U.S. vessels, one-third to Soviet vessels, and one-third to foreign flag vessels. But whereas the Russians agreed to pay the market rate plus 10 percent, with an $8.05 a ton minimum, they claimed that the world market rate was $7.50 a ton; the U.S. Maritime Administration said it was closer to $10.35 a ton; adding the 10 percent surcharges, the difference was $8.25 versus $11.38.

Since the Russians had probably bought about 18 million tons of U.S. grain and oilseeds, and 6 million were to go in U.S. vessels, the $3-plus discrepancy in freight rates could mean a difference of $18 million in shipping costs to be borne by the U.S.S.R. (As it turned out, many U.S. shipowners declined their option to carry the Soviet grain; their vessels were more profitably employed carrying other cargo. Thus much less than a third of the grain ended up going in U.S. vessels.)

Not until November 22 did Moscow and Washington see eye to eye. Under an agreement signed by Robert J. Blackwell, assistant secretary of commerce for maritime affairs, and Nikolai Zuev, president of the Soviet shipping agency Sovfracht, Moscow would pay rates averaging $10.12 a ton through January 25, 1973. Within a month the agreement was amended to make the rate $10.34 a ton between January 26 and July 1. The rates included a premium for U.S. ship operators designed to reduce the operating subsidies paid to them.

Ships used for transporting grain are often tankers, the same tankers used to carry Kuwait oil, liquefied natural gas, and California wine. Many are supertankers that can carry hundreds of thousands of tons, ships too big for the Suez Canal but so automated, so efficient that if the Suez Canal were to reopen tomorrow, it would have nothing like its old traffic. Like the Suez, Soviet ports are not equipped to handle supertankers of much over 100,000 tons.

The Baltic Exchange deals mostly in "spot," or single journey, charters. In late 1972, Sovfracht was booking tankers on time charters, which run for a year and more, through firms in New York, Tokyo, and other cities rather than through London. Instead of paying so much a ton to ship grain from U.S. Gulf ports to the Black Sea or to Baltic ports, Sovfracht was evidently prepared to pay for one- and two-year periods and to use the ships for as many voyages as possible in that time, or perhaps simply as storage depots. The Chinese, too, were booking tankers on time charter, and the competition for oceangoing carriers was raising world shipping rates.

Some doubts were raised as to the Soviets' ability to ship and store all the grain they had bought and were entitled to transport in Soviet bottoms. Only a small percentage of the huge Soviet merchant fleet is equipped to carry grain in optimum conditions of dryness. Nor does the U.S.S.R. have the grain storage capacity found in the United States and Canada. Before it can be stored, damp grain must be dried, and most of the Soviet Union's drying machines are in Siberia. Damp grain would have to be shipped by rail to Siberia, and then shipped back after drying to European Russia.

Odessa, the great Black Sea port 7,000 miles from Houston and other large U.S. Gulf ports, received her first American grain ship on December 20, although some U.S. grain had arrived earlier aboard foreign-flag vessels.

Almost immediately upon arrival, the *Ogden Willamette,* with 36,500 tons of wheat and a crew of thirty-three, was boarded by forty Soviet stevedores. They used sixteen American-made pneumatic suction machines—"Vac-u-vators"—to blow wheat into boxcars lined up on sidings at the port.

Within a few days the *Ogden Willamette* was followed by the *National Defender,* carrying 54,000 tons of wheat, and the *Overseas Joyce,* with 47,500 tons. These were the first U.S. ships to dock in a Soviet port since 1964.

The *Overseas Aleutian,* which arrived on December 30 with 37,000 tons of grain, was dispatched after unloading to the Black Sea ports of Batum and Tuapse, in the Georgian Republic. There she was loaded with 244,500 barrels of No. 2 heating oil to be delivered in New York and Boston. To relieve growing fuel shortages in the Northeast, the White House had removed a ruling that No. 2 fuel could be imported only from Western Hemisphere sources.

Measured against the 20 million barrels of fuel oil the United States was refining each week, the amount imported from the U.S.S.R. was a drop in the bucket. But it did show that East-West trade could be a two-way proposition.

To men with long memories, it was a reminder of how much the world had changed since the summer of

1964, when the captain of the U.S. tanker *Sister Katingo* charged that a Soviet ship in the Black Sea off Novorossisk had fired three warning shots across his bow after a dispute over unloading fees. When Russian stevedores were called off the job, the captain had ordered his crew to unload the 32,436-ton cargo. That was evidently what had provoked the Russian warning. Soviet sailors had boarded and searched his ship, the captain said, and had used other "excessive" methods before releasing it. Moscow rejected a U.S. protest, insisted that only flares had been fired, and banned the ship's captain from Soviet ports. Interviewed later in Port Said, the skipper said he had seen the very thing Secretary Rusk had warned against—Cuba-bound ships being loaded with U.S. grain. Moscow denied the charge.

Now the atmosphere was far more relaxed. Shipowners stood to profit by the easing of trade relations. They could also look forward to receiving subsidies on their grain shipments to the Soviet Union. Operating subsidies paid by the U.S. Maritime Administration are based on the competitive cost disadvantages a U.S. shipowner suffers as compared with a foreign shipowner, who does not have to pay his crews such high wages. The subsidies are also based on factors that vary from one ship to another; some vessels are larger, newer, carry smaller crews, have lower insurance costs, and require less maintenance and repair, which puts them in a better competitive position vis-à-vis foreign ships; the lower their operating costs, the smaller the amount for which they are eligible in operating subsidies.

In the maritime agreement with Moscow signed October 14, it was assumed that 19.2 million tons of U.S. grain and soybeans would be shipped, a figure that came just a shade short of the 19.25 million Exportkhleb probably bought. American shipowners were to be given the opportunity to carry 6.4 million tons, one third the total. An official "give-up" of 570,000 tons in December reduced the U.S. share to about 5.8 million tons maximum, and in the budget Richard Nixon submitted to Congress on January 29, 1973, the probable figure was lowered to 5.689 million tons. It would be further reduced as shipowners declined their options to carry Soviet grain.

A shipowner is eligible for subsidy on a voyage only after his vessel returns to a U.S. port; the Maritime Administration must audit all the costs of the voyage before he receives his subsidy check. At roughly $9.69 per ton, owners of U.S. tankers and bulk carriers transporting grain to Russian ports would receive about $55 million in operating subsidies. (Had the grain been shipped at the lower tonnage rates that the Russians originally demanded, the subsidies would have been higher.) Since nearly half the voyages would not be completed with costs audited by the end of the fiscal year on June 30, about $28 million was allocated for subsidy payments in 1973. Operating subsidies for all U.S. ships in fiscal 1973 were projected at $215 million, of which the subsidies on the grain shipments amounted to less than 13 percent.

Just how much more it cost the Russians to ship some of their purchase in U.S. bottoms rather than in foreign bottoms—the great bone of contention that held up shipments until early December—is hard to calculate, just as it is hard to calculate the world freight rate. Both are subject to argument. Taxpayers might cavil at paying $55 million in operating subsidies to shipowners carrying Soviet grain, but it is hard to prove the ships would not have received subsidies carrying other cargo to different destinations, or that the subsidies would not have been larger.

7.

Except for the Russians, who bought a quarter of the 1972 U.S. wheat crop at fire-sale prices, almost nobody was altogether happy about the massive sales of wheat.

Farmers in Texas, Oklahoma, and southern Kansas complained that nobody had told them the Russians might buy; they had lost millions, they said, by selling to cooperative and independent elevators when the market was still low.

Some country elevator operators who had not bought wheat futures to hedge their sales to exporters were forced into bankruptcy and thus reneged on contracts they had made with exporters.

Consumer activists charged that U.S. taxpayers, through export subsidies paid to trading companies, had actually subsidized the Russians.

Bakers went out of business partly because they could not raise prices to compensate for the increased cost of flour.

When bread prices did begin to rise early in 1973, consumers blamed the price hikes on the sales of wheat to

Russia. They also blamed subsidies to wheat farmers. And they welcomed indications that Richard Nixon was trying to scale down the subsidies.

U.S. farm subsidies date back to 1933, when they were established, under Franklin Roosevelt's New Deal, to support farmers' incomes, to encourage farmers to remain farmers, and to discourage the overproduction that was making it unprofitable to till the land.

Even in the booming 1920s, the farmers had been in trouble. More than a quarter of Americans still lived on or from the farm; few of them lived well. When wheat had jumped to $2.20 a bushel in World War I, farmers plowed new cropland, and much of it was still in production. Now, with exports dropping to less than half their 1919 level, more than a billion acres were still being worked. Commodity prices sank, and farm income sank along with them. Average farm income in 1930 was only $400 per family. Not $400 a week or even $400 a month— $400 a year. And if that was the average, millions of farm families earned even less, although subsistence farmers lived mainly outside the money economy.

While Ukrainians died of famine in 1931, Americans harvested a record wheat crop. That dropped wheat prices to new lows, and many Kansas counties declared a moratorium on taxes to help farmers survive. The Great Depression was tightening its squeeze in the cities, where jobless workers could not afford to buy the farmers' produce. Congress authorized the Federal Farm Board to distribute 85 million bushels of wheat to the needy through the Red Cross, and as breadlines formed in the cities nearly a million Americans went back to the land. Operating farms actually increased in number from 6.3 million in 1930 to 7.2 million in 1931. But even subsistence farmers were barely subsisting.

Never before in the nation's history had so many Americans been so ill-fed. An Agricultural Marketing Act signed by President Hoover in 1929 had authorized a stabilization corporation, but prices were still falling. The free crop market was just not working, and the new administration of Franklin Roosevelt could hardly sit by and let people starve.

Along with programs that made jobs, Roosevelt asked Congress to enact massive legislation that would restore farm income, partly by raising commodity prices to the average levels they had held in the pre-World War I years of 1910 to 1914.

In June, 1933, Roosevelt's "Emergency Farm Bill" became law, setting up the Agricultural Adjustment Administration (AAA). But most crops had already been planted, pigs had been farrowed, and Agriculture Secretary Henry A. Wallace ordered the immediate slaughter of 400,000 baby pigs and the plowing under of some crops, mostly cotton.

Much of the invective hurled at That Man in the White House arose from the horror of seeing baby pigs sacrificed to raise farm incomes, and at seeing food prices rise in city markets. The acreage allotments imposed on farmers under the AAA to limit their production of major crops such as wheat and feed grains were attacked as unconstitutional.

And if farmers were anguished by some of the New Deal's measures to help them, their despair was soon deepened by a scorching drought; in many parts of the country it was the most severe and prolonged drought in memory. Land plowed during World War I to plant crops was turning to dust in the second summer of the New Deal. On May 12, 1934, the precise anniversary of the Farm Act's passage in Congress, a dust storm swept east like a Biblical omen to darken the sun above New York, Washington, Baltimore, and Philadelphia, and to dirty windowsills on its way out to sea.

Some 300 million tons of Arkansas, Colorado, Kansas, Oklahoma, and Texas topsoil blew into the Atlantic Ocean in 1934. And the first of 350,000 "Arkies" and "Okies," memorialized later by John Steinbeck in *The Grapes of Wrath*, began their trek from the Dust Bowl west to California.

Drought more than government planting restrictions held down farm production in 1935, and when the Supreme Court early in 1936 struck down parts of the 1933 Agricultural Adjustment Act as unconstitutional, soil conservation served as the ostensible basis for a new effort to limit the size of crops. A third of U.S. farmers had been receiving government acreage allotment checks for not growing crops; now Henry Wallace instituted a stopgap scheme under which farmers were paid to plant soil-conserving crops such as alfalfa, clover, and lespedeza instead of soil-depleting crops such as corn, cotton, tobacco, and wheat.

Kansas farmers fought tooth and nail against government "meddling," but the majority of Americans were finding hope in the New Deal solutions. Industrial earnings were up, and people were eating more red meat (especially beef and pork), more dairy products, more fruits and vegetables (although Americans still ate only 50 million chickens a year, as compared with more than 2½ billion today).

When Republican Alfred M. Landon of Kansas ran for the presidency in 1936, he fared even worse than Democrat George McGovern did three dozen years later.

Roosevelt's second term began as the drought ended. And by February 16, 1938, a revised Triple-A not only relaxed restrictions of most major crop plantings but even supplied farmers with lime and mineral fertilizers to help them achieve greater crop yields to the acre. Pare Lorentz, when he filmed his classic documentary *The Plow That Broke the Plains* in 1936, had found the plains parched and the farmers gloomy. Now things were looking up.

It was the 1938 Agricultural Adjustment Act that began direct crop-subsidy payments, the so-called parity payments. The Act also set up the Commodity Credit Corporation (CCC) that could support farm prices by buying up surpluses to be stored in an "Ever-Normal Granary" to protect the country against drought and plant disease. (Rust, as it happened, reduced the 1938 wheat crop by 100 million bushels.) The CCC could also distribute surpluses to needy families through state welfare agencies and the Food Stamp Plan, which first went into effect in Rochester, New York, in May, 1939. This plan virtually subsidized low-income consumers, enabling them to buy surplus food products at a discount.

To protect wheat farmers from their own ruinous tendency to overproduce, Agriculture Secretary Wallace set up a quota system. Farmers were assigned acreage allotments, and when Washington predicted a surplus for the upcoming year, farmers with allotments voted on whether quotas should be established; if two-thirds or more approved the marketing quota, then everybody had to go along. A farmer without a wheat acreage allotment was not permitted to plant more than fifteen acres in wheat.

Along with its new leverage to hold down production, the USDA now employed export subsidies to help dispose of surpluses. Little more than 3 million tons of U.S. wheat were exported in the crop year ending June 30, 1939, but it was a beginning. (The government paid about 27.4 cents a bushel in export subsidy on most of that wheat.)

By 1940, about 160 million acres, one-sixth of the land cultivated in 1930, had been withdrawn from production. But what really raised farm incomes in 1940 was higher prices, lifted by the demands of a war-ravaged Europe, and increased output per acre of land, especially in the Corn Belt.

Golden Cross Bantam corn had been first planted on a commercial scale in 1933 and higher-yielding hybrid corn was now being planted throughout the Corn Belt. Sulfanomide drugs, first used in 1935, were now in wide use against livestock and poultry diseases. Combines were replacing threshing machines. Aerial crop-dusting, first tried experimentally in Maine in 1932, was coming into favor. Improved fertilizers, pesticides, animal health products, and farm equipment were revolutionizing U.S. agriculture.

In 1860 a farm worker produced only enough food and fiber for 4.5 people. By 1900 he could produce enough for 7 people; by 1950 enough for 15. And in the 1950s and 1960s the farmer's productivity grew like the corn in August. By 1963 he was turning out enough for 31 people; by 1972 enough for 50 (while his Russian counterpart still produced only enough for 7). His output per hour was six times what it had been in 1920. Crop yield per acre and output per breeding animal had more than doubled since 1930; on less than 40 percent of the land cultivated then, America now produced a lot more food.

Less than 5 percent of the U.S. work force remained on the farm (as compared with 33 percent in the U.S.S.R.), and the productivity of farm workers, already high at the start of the 1960s, had for a decade increased each year at twice the rate of industrial workers.

Agricultural efficiency had pushed a million people a year off the land in the 1950s and 1960s, shoving them into the cities where their lack of industrial skills aggravated problems of urban unemployment and welfare, drug abuse, and crime.

Some farm efficiency was achieved at the expense of the environment.

And because of efficiency in food production, some American foods suffered in quality. Chicken lacked flavor; many fruits and vegetables were grown from varieties selected more for harvesting and marketing expediency than for taste; "battery" hens did not lay eggs with quite the savor of those from the old backyard hens of the farmer's wife.

Still, U.S. farm efficiency was the marvel of the world, and in some cases its salvation. Without that efficiency, U.S. supermarket prices would have been astronomical.

A favorite target among angry supermarket patrons in 1973 was agribusiness.

Rich corporate farms were charged with degrading the taste of food and with accounting for so much farm output that they were in a position to influence food prices.

Populists as early as the 1880s had backed legislation, some of it still on the books in Kansas, North Dakota, and Oklahoma, that prohibited corporations from owning land. John Kennedy's agriculture secretary, Orville Freeman, fretting about corporate farms, ordered a study made: it showed that only 1 percent of all farms representing less than 7 percent of the nation's farmland was owned by corporations.

Farm ownership, nevertheless, has become more and more concentrated, and although agriculture in America is still almost entirely in the hands of individual farmers, many of those farmers have enormous investments in land, buildings, equipment, and livestock. They may have muddy boots and callused hands, but they are among the richest capitalists in the world.

The 1931 days of 7.2 million farms are long gone; the country now has about 2.8 million farms and they average less than 400 acres each. But most of the small farms are part-time operations whose farmers also hold down non-farm jobs. It takes more acreage, more livestock, more equipment to operate an economically viable farm today. About 55,000 farms, less than 2 percent of the total number, now sell a third of all agricultural products. These superfarms are not the traditional diversified farms, able to respond nimbly to changes in market prices; they are specialized grain farms, hog farms, or cattle farms. Many are owned by corporate stockholders (though often the stockholders are related); they average $100,000 or more per year in cash receipts.

Just over one-fifth of the nation's farms account for nearly four-fifths of all cash receipts from farming. These farms average $20,000 each in gross income, including subsidies.

The embattled yeoman dirt farmer hangs on, but he no longer accounts for the lion's share of America's food production, and food prices have not gone down as his ranks have thinned. Diversified corporations and rich nonfarm investors have been favored by depreciation and capital gains provisions in the tax laws, while inheritance taxes have worked to break up family farms; processing companies have not been required to bargain collectively with cooperatives of small farmers; agricultural research and farm subsidy programs have given priority to larger, more prosperous farming enterprises.

One-fifth of U.S. farms, about 618,000 in all, receive

three-fifths of all direct government subsidy payments.

In the years since 1933, about $50 billion has been paid in direct farm subsidies. In 1972 alone, farmers pocketed about $4 billion in subsidy money, which represented more than a fifth of their net income. About $855 million went to wheat farmers, who would have received even more had not so much of their wheat been sold at such fat prices.

So many complaints are heard about farm subsidies that a supermarket customer had better understand how the subsidy, specifically the wheat subsidy, actually works.

It takes a good head for figures to be a farmer in America, and it takes a patience for tortuous arithmetic to appreciate the options open to a farmer in planting and selling his crop. If his crop is wheat, one must bear in mind that about half the U.S. wheat crop is grown for export, and almost a fifth for seed and feed. In theory, a wheat farmer receives subsidy only on the portion of his crop intended for domestic food consumption. (In practice, of course, he has no control over the disposition of his wheat after he sells it, but subsidy is computed on the basis of about one-third the nation's crop.)

A wheat farmer need not participate in the subsidy program. Under the Agricultural Act of 1970, which applies to crops through 1973, a farmer who chooses not to participate may plant all the wheat he wants; in that case, however, he is not eligible for benefits under the program.

If he does participate, he agrees to plant in wheat a share of the acreage the USDA deems necessary to assure an adequate supply of wheat for U.S. flour consumption.* In addition, he agrees to set aside wheat cropland equal

---

* 18.7 million acres are needed to grow 535 million bushels (14.6 million tons).

to a predetermined percentage of his allotment acreage (83 percent in 1972). He may put this land into summer fallow or put it to conservation uses such as planting it in grasses or legumes, small grain cover crops, trees, or plantings for wildlife food and cover. He agrees to protect his set-aside acreage against erosion, insect damage, rodents, and weeds.

So long as he complies with the set-aside and conservation rules, he is entitled to subsidy payments, even if he plants no wheat at all or loses the crop he plants. The subsidy is designed to bring him 100 percent of parity on his share of the total crop grown for use in U.S. food.

We have used that word parity without defining it. Parity is the amount a farmer should receive in today's dollars for his grain, his hogs, his milk, his eggs, his apples, his steers, his cotton, his potatoes, his tobacco, or his soybeans if he is to enjoy the same standard of living farmers enjoyed in the United States between 1910 and 1914, as established by the New Deal's AAA.

If and when a wheat farmer harvests his crop (and he must plant wheat or an acceptable substitute to maintain his allotment), and stores it in his own bins or in a grain elevator, he is eligible for a federal loan of roughly $1.25 per bushel. Come what may, then, he is guaranteed a minimum of $1.25 per bushel for his crop. He can now sell his crop to the Commodity Credit Corporation at $1.25, with some adjustments; or he can take $1.25 per bushel as a loan and store his crop, hoping the price of wheat will go up enough before he sells it to cover his storage costs.

A farmer outside Mankato, Kansas (let's call him Werner Schmidt) has 100 acres in wheat. His domestic prorated allotment in 1972 was 30 acres, which meant he had to set aside 24.9 acres (83% x 30). On his remaining 75.1 acres he averaged thirty bushels of wheat per acre.

As of July 1, 1972, the parity price of wheat was tentatively computed at $3.02 per bushel—the price wheat would have to fetch for a wheat farmer to match the standard of living farmers enjoyed in the five years before World War I.

What Schmidt actually received when he sold his crop in August was $1.68 per bushel; that happened to be the average national price of wheat received by farmers in the first five months of the crop year, July to November, 1972. Since the price was 43 cents above the loan level, Werner Schmidt was not complaining.

The $1.68 price was a surprise not only to Schmidt but to the USDA, which had expected wheat to average about $1.30 a bushel as it had in the same period of 1971. In fact, the government had sent Schmidt a subsidy check in early July based on that anticipation. The amount of the check was calculated on what the USDA calls a certificate value, which is the difference between the parity price and the actual price. The difference between parity ($3.02) and about $1.30 would be about $1.72.

Nobody can know the average July-November price until the end of November, but by law the USDA pays 75 percent of the certificate value in advance. Schmidt could expect his remaining 25 percent in early December.

If the USDA's prediction of $1.30 as an average price had been on target, Schmidt's December check would have been $387.* But wheat prices went so high in 1972 that the certificate value, instead of being $1.72, as the USDA had estimated, came to only $1.34. And Schmidt's check, instead of being for $387, was for a disappointing $85.50.

Farmers in Texas and Oklahoma, who complained

---

* Schmidt was entitled to subsidy on 900 bushels—30 allotment acres × 30 bushels per acre. At $1.72 per bushel his total subsidy came to $1,548 —of which 75 percent of the anticipated total, $1,161, was paid in July and the remaining 25 percent, $387, was due in December.

with keen hindsight that they had sold at \$1.32 a bushel and then had watched wheat prices soar, in some cases sued the Department of Agriculture and the export companies. But Werner Schmidt, even with his reduced subsidy payment, had done well. His 75.1 acres had yielded over \$4,990, almost \$600 more—even with a lower subsidy—than he had earned for the same amount of wheat the year before.

By increasing the average price of U.S. wheat in 1972, the Russian purchases not only benefitted most wheat farmers but saved U.S. taxpayers more than \$200 million in subsidies that would otherwise have been payable to wheat farmers.

Moscow's buying did something else: it sparked hopes by some people, including Richard Nixon, that the entire subsidy program might be junked, or at least severely modified.

Of all the subsidies paid to farmers, the wheat subsidy was unique.

Corn farmers receive subsidy, soybean farmers receive subsidy, but consumers of beef, chicken, pork, milk, and eggs, all produced largely from corn- and soybean-fed animals and poultry, have not had to bear the direct cost of the corn or soybean subsidy.

Cotton planters receive subsidy, but a man who wears cotton shirts or a woman who wears cotton dresses has not paid a premium to help cover the cost of the cotton subsidy.

Since 1964, the subsidy to wheat farmers had been recovered in part from flour millers. The miller had to pay the government 75 cents for every bushel of wheat he ground. And since the miller passed this cost on to the consumer with every bag of flour—or to the baker or pasta maker who then passed it on to the consumer—the flour buyer, the bread buyer, the pasta buyer was singled out to help bear the cost of the wheat subsidy.

A bushel of wheat yields enough flour for about sixty-nine loaves of bread, so the bread buyer paid just over a penny extra per one-pound loaf to subsidize the farmer.

Whether or not farmers should be subsidized was not the issue here. Applying the farmer's subsidy directly to the price of flour, bread, macaroni, or crackers was what economists call "regressive" taxation; unlike the income tax, which graduates according to people's ability to pay, a sales tax like the tax on bread and macaroni takes its biggest bite from those least able to pay, those who spent the largest share of their income on food.

A Republican congressman from Illinois, Paul Findley, introduced legislation early in 1973 that would abolish the "bread tax" of 75 cents per bushel on wheat used domestically for food. Other lawmakers proposed or supported such reform, which was finally achieved in the four-year farm program signed into law by Richard Nixon on August 10. It would save bread buyers and other flour-product consumers as much as $400 million a year.

But this tax accounted for only a tiny part of the cost of a loaf of bread.

What gobbles up most of the consumer's bread money is distribution. To move a loaf of bread from a bakery in Chicago to a local supermarket in Evanston costs more than it does to grow the wheat in Kansas, take it to a miller in Buffalo, grind the wheat into flour, and take the flour to the Chicago bakery.

Much of the high delivery cost is rooted in the percentage system under which driver-salesmen are paid. The men are members of the Teamsters Union. Under his union contract, a driver-salesman in a metropolitan area typically gets $116 a week in base pay (plus or minus $10 depending on location); in addition, he gets 8½ percent commission on all his sales (the figure varies from 8 percent in some places to 10 percent in others).

On a typical $2,000 route, a driver-salesman makes about $300 a week, plus fringe benefits. If the price of bread goes up, he gets a windfall. His increased take has to be added to what the grocer pays, and since the profit margin tacked on by the grocer is computed on his cost, the price to the consumer goes up out of all proportion to the penny or two extra the baker may charge to recover his higher flour cost.

Even in some areas where the volume of business is so high the baker delivers in tractor-trailers, paying drivers on an hourly basis, the driver-salesman whose accounts are serviced this way, although he contributes nothing to the delivery, receives full commission under the terms of his union contract. Bakers in some parts of the country are trying to change this system; the Teamsters Union works to keep it as is.

Meanwhile, a rise in the price of wheat, which increases the price of flour, is only the beginning of a chain reaction down the line of distribution that profits driver-salesmen but squeezes the bread-buying public.

8.

These complexities of the capitalist system, both in production and distribution, are an abomination to the Communists. But in terms of feeding the Russian people, Communism does not have a proud history.

If agriculture was inefficient under the Czars, it became even less efficient under the Communists. For all the Marxist rhetoric about the industrial proletariat, the masses who provided the Revolution's main support were the peasants; in 1917 those sons of serfs grabbed their landlords' fields (Lenin could not have stopped them if he had tried), and the trouble started right there. The peasants proved inept farmers and worse managers. Farm production fell, food supplies dwindled.

Agriculture in fact was the paramount problem of the Soviet economy almost from the start, partly because only about 10 percent of the country's land is suitable for farming (and even much of that is second-rate farmland), partly because Marx, Lenin, Trotsky, and Stalin were basically city men.

Lenin in 1920 appealed to the American Communist Party for a report on U.S. agriculture to be used as a guide for Russia. Harold M. Ware, an American Communist who had graduated from an agricultural college in Pennsylvania, made a six-month tour of farms in the South, the Midwest, the Northwest; he sent a report direct to Lenin. A year later, taking an active role in the Society of Friends of Soviet Russia, he accompanied the journalist Lincoln Steffens on a lecture tour of the United States, rallying support and sympathy for the Bolsheviks, who were now in the throes of a terrible famine.

Steffens was president of a famine relief group, and Ware persuaded him to turn over $70,000 in lecture fees to buy tractors and other farm equipment for a group of volunteers to instruct Russians in mechanized agriculture. Russia had fewer than 1,500 tractors of its own, and many of these were unrepairable wrecks.

A good many Americans were flocking to Russia in those days, some of them Communists or Socialists, some apolitical adventurers, some humanitarians, some simply capitalists looking for profits. Moscow discouraged naïve immigrants motivated by superficial idealism. Radio broadcasts in 1920 warned that living conditions were rough in Russia and asked that would-be immigrants enter only in organized groups. Lenin told foreign workers they must come bringing enough food, clothing, and other necessities to last them at least two years, and that was before the famine.

Harold Ware's volunteers, all farmers and mechanics, went to Russia in the spring of 1922 with twenty-one tractors, some other machinery, seeds, and a large amount of food and other supplies. Assigned to lands of an abandoned monastery near Perm, in the Urals, where there was acute hunger and suffering, the Americans used their tractors as bait to induce the peasants to give up their small holdings and join collectives.

Early in August, 1922, exactly fifty years before Nikolai Belousov completed his purchase of U.S. grain, Harold Ware's U.S. tractors were turning their first furrows on the monastery land while thousands of peasants from miles around tugged at their beards in wonder. The Americans seeded most of 4,000 acres in winter wheat and returned to America.

For the next two years Ware solicited money and support for a campaign to mechanize Soviet agriculture. He raised $150,000, organized a group of twenty-six volunteers, and went back to Russia in the spring of 1925. On 15,000 acres of fertile but abandoned earth in the Kuban area of the northern Caucasus, he demonstrated mechanized farming to more Russian peasants.

Moscow chose this prototype Peace Corpsman to oversee a program of organizing huge, mechanized state farms throughout the Soviet Union, which Ware did until 1932. He was also a dollar-a-year man for the U.S. Department of Agriculture.

Best known of the U.S. humanitarians was Herbert C. Hoover, Warren Harding's secretary of commerce whose American Relief Administration, responding to an appeal by the writer Maxim Gorky, spent more than $60 million on famine relief to Russia in the years from 1921 to 1923. The program of food shipments and medical aid was credited with saving the lives of 10 million Russians, more than a third of them children.

"American aid," said Gorky in a letter to Hoover at the end of the program, "will long remain in the memory of millions of Russian children whom you saved from death."

Lenin granted concessions to foreigners to enlist their

help in rehabilitating the Soviet economy. One of the first concessions was granted to the Allied Drug and Chemical Corporation, headed by a young American physician, fresh out of Columbia University Medical School. (Half a century later, as chairman of the Occidental Petroleum Corporation of Los Angeles, Dr. Armand Hammer was once again in Moscow, this time negotiating for Soviet petroleum and natural gas.)

Hammer not only helped to reestablish Soviet asbestos mining but also won Lenin's gratitude and friendship by arranging the purchase of thousands of tons of U.S. wheat to feed starving Russians; in exchange for the wheat, the Kremlin traded furs, hides, and art treasures (which formed the basis of a private collection donated by Armand Hammer to the University of Southern California in 1965, and of the Hammer Galleries in New York).

Ware and Hammer (who with his brother Victor netted several million dollars from the asbestos venture and from a Moscow pencil factory) were not alone. Other Americans—engineers and workers—helped Russians, Ukrainians, and other Soviet citizens, many of them illiterate peasants fresh from the fields, to build a tractor factory in Kharkov and to master complex machines and production techniques, including the assembly-line system of mass production. The plant, which still stands, turned out its first tractor in the fall of 1931 and reached its planned volume of 100 a day by May, 1932. By 1936 its output was up to 145 a day. The Americans left after one year, but the factory still produces tractors. Another factory, at Stalingrad (now Volgograd), manufactured a fifteen-horsepower tractor designed by the International Harvester Company of Chicago, founded by Cyrus McCormick of reaper fame. It was a primitive machine, but Russian peasants took off their hats and stood in awe when one sputtered into a village. Its arrival was greeted with brass bands, banners, and throngs of peasants; few men dared to clamber onto the steel seat and learn how to operate the machine.

Russian agriculture remained largely primitive. When Josef Stalin came to power in 1926, he found himself thwarted by the power of backward rural Russia. Except for a few large state-operated grain and cattle farms, most of them estates the Bolsheviks had appropriated, and a handful of cooperative farms, agriculture was still in the hands of individual peasants. Not only did they resist modern methods, they could exert tremendous pressure on the government by reducing the amount of land they planted or by withholding food from the market.

Stalin determined to break their power, to wrest more profit for the state from agriculture, and to raise farm output by pooling peasant plots into large, well-managed, efficient state farms and collectives. Stalin's first Five-Year Plan, begun in October, 1928, shipped millions of rich peasants (kulaks) to Siberia. Many resisted; they slaughtered their livestock, burned their crops, hid their grain from the state collectors. Millions were ruthlessly liquidated. And within less than three years more than 95 percent of Russia's farmland was incorporated in state and collective farms.

The results were disastrous. The Russian farmers stubbornly defied efforts to increase production. About 20 percent of the Siberian wheat crop succumbed to rust in 1932, but the grim famine of the early 1930s struck hardest in the Ukraine and the north Caucasus; a major cause was the new Soviet agrarian policies. Moscow did its best to conceal Russia's famine from the world; it reduced the amount of foodstuffs taken by the state from collective farms and permitted the farms to sell part of their surplus produce.

But Stalinist farm policies crippled Soviet food production. Stalin reportedly acknowledged that fact during World War II when he confessed to Winston Churchill that he regretted his program of collectivization, which later produced wartime food shortages. Russians died of starvation in the years from 1941 to 1945, and not just those Russians who were besieged at Leningrad and Stalingrad. The effects of the Stalinist agricultural programs were still being felt in the 1960s. Perhaps even in the 1970s.

Unlike Stalin, who gave top priority to heavy industry, Nikita S. Khrushchev emphasized agriculture, although much of his interest may have been in boosting efficiency simply to release some of the vast rural labor pool for urban industrial jobs.

In 1957, Khrushchev startled the world when he demonstrated Soviet technological capability with the sputnik, man's first space satellite. But some Russians grumbled. "Better to learn to feed your people at home before starting to explore the moon," said one Russian quoted by Harrison Salisbury of *The New York Times.*

Khrushchev tried hard. He revealed that Soviet agriculture had produced little more in 1952 than it had in 1916, the last year of Czarist rule. And he took steps to improve matters.

Khrushchev visited Iowa. He came back from Roswell Garst's farm in Coon Rapids with pleas that more productive crops be planted. What their country needed, he told Soviet leaders, was more extensive application of chemical fertilizers, more pesticides, more mechanization. He made Russia the world's biggest tractor maker. He increased substantially the take-home pay of farm workers.

And he sowed to grain nearly 100 million acres of virgin lands in Siberia and Kazakhstan, lands previously considered too dry to plow lest they end up as a Soviet dust bowl.

By 1965, Khrushchev promised, the Soviet Union would overtake the United States in production of meat, milk, and butter, and Russia's standard of living would equal or exceed America's by 1970 or 1975.

Only in the world's richer countries do people consume any great quantities of meat, milk, butter, poultry, and eggs. A country's living standards are commonly judged on the basis of its animal protein consumption, and the U.S.S.R., although rich, has always been short of these foods. Khrushchev would make them plentiful.

But in 1961 and 1962, meat, eggs, and butter were scarce as hens' teeth in Moscow and other large Soviet cities. Milk was available only for nursing mothers and small children. Populations had increased, urban purchasing power had risen, but food production had failed to keep pace. Except in some peasant farmers' markets, where prices were exorbitant, Russian housewives found no meat except occasional sausages and canned meats.

Under Stalin such shortages had been borne stolidly; now, in de-Stalinized Russia, people complained. For generations they had given up all the amenities of life to build for the future; now they were tired of sacrifices, and of promises.

In 1963 the Communist Party Central Committee said that Stalin had caused many deaths in 1947 by exporting grain even in poor crop years. So poor were Soviet crops in 1963 that Russia was obliged to come to the capitalist, imperialist nations of the West for the food it needed to survive.

Most of the wheat came from Canada. Muscovites joked bitterly about that.

"Comrade Khrushchev has performed a miracle; he has sown wheat in Kazakhstan and reaped it in Canada." An official in Kazakhstan said that the crop there had amounted to only 5 million tons, with the yield less than five bushels per acre. Khrushchev himself was so depressed he declared the ten-year Kazakhstan program a failure; the new lands had contributed only 35 percent of Russia's marketable grain, and wheat-growing would be ended in the region. (He soon changed his mind and the 1964 crop in Kazakhstan set records.)

America's military-industrial complex has its counterpart in the Soviet Union; "metal eaters," Khrushchev called them. Khrushchev could not stand up to his metal eaters any more than Lyndon Johnson or Richard Nixon could stand up to theirs, and in 1959 and 1960 the Soviet power lobby made demands that forced Khrushchev to cut agricultural budgets in order to increase defense outlays. Khrushchev said late in 1963 that a new program to expand Soviet fertilizer output would double the nation's crops by 1970, but although Armand Hammer announced a trade deal in 1964 that would enable him to build two Soviet fertilizer plants the plants never got built. It was partly an order of priorities oriented toward the metal eaters that was responsible for the Russian food shortage and Khrushchev's downfall.

Part of that food shortage came from severe restrictions imposed by Khrushchev on private farm plots. These plots represent altogether only 3 percent of the country's total cultivated area; they average only half an acre in size. But a peasant on a private farm is permitted to own a cow, chickens, a few pigs, and some sheep on his land;

half of Russia's eggs, a third of her meat and milk, 38 percent of her vegetables, and 63 percent of her potatoes reportedly come from peasants' private plots.

In Moscow's Central Market, even in the dead of winter, citizens can buy apples, fresh cucumbers, eggs, persimmons, pomegranates, poppy seeds, raisins, sauerkraut, shelled walnuts, tangerines, and wild mushrooms. Any of these foods that may come from the 32,800 large collective farms or the 15,500 much larger state farms will inevitably cost less than foods grown on private plots, but they must go through the elaborate marketing apparatus that diminishes their quality. Just as some Americans pay premium prices for "organically" grown produce, the costlier, fresher produce grown privately is preferred in Russia and other Eastern bloc countries.

Restrictions on private farming were relaxed somewhat after Khrushchev was ousted from power in 1964. But collectivization cannot be called a major obstacle to production in Communist agriculture; for grain crops it has probably been no hindrance at all. Other factors must be taken into account. As the Party newspaper *Pravda* noted in late January, 1973, "the struggle for a good harvest is waged not only in the fields" but in factories and supply organizations as well. For spring planting in 1973, *Pravda* said, Soviet farmers would need 48,000 new tractorized sowers, 53,000 cultivators, 18,000 fertilizer spreaders, and "many thousands" of other pieces of equipment. Plants in Altai, Chelyabinsk, Kharkov, Minsk, and Riga were producing at a good pace, but at a factory in Novosibirsk, scheduled to turn out 22,000 sowers in 1973, production was "lackadaisical."

Private agriculture is not necessarily more productive than state agriculture. In Poland, farmers resisted collectivization so stoutly that efforts to collectivize them were finally reversed in 1956. But although 90 percent of the land is privately owned in Poland, and private farmers account for 87 percent of the nation's produce, food production in Poland has still fallen far short of the people's demands.

This shortage, by contributing to the 1970 riots that so rocked the Kremlin, led to the redoubling of Russian efforts to increase their own food production. To enlarge their livestock and poultry holdings, the Soviets needed feed grain. From buying U.S. corn in 1971 it was but a short step to buying U.S. wheat in 1972.

9.

Those who profited most by the colossal Soviet grain and soybean purchases were those few market speculators who bought commodity futures at the right time and held them long enough.

Someone who bought ten contracts of wheat and held them while the market climbed a full dizzying dollar could have seen an investment of $6,000 appreciate to $56,000.

The question is, would this imaginary winner profit only at the expense of those who sold wheat short, or would he profit also at the expense of the food-buying public?

Early in 1973, three Washington correspondents of the *Des Moines Register* collaborated on a six-part series about the regulation of commodity trading. There were strong indications, they said, that the markets are often "rigged." And that futures prices can affect the real prices of supermarket foods.

Representative Neal Smith, a Democratic Congressman from Iowa, has called commodity trading "the biggest legal gambling game in the world." The game, says

Representative Smith, is crooked. Commodity speculators, he claims, "get together on the trading floor every morning and talk among themselves and decide whether the market is going to go up or down that day. Then they start buying. They don't care about supply and demand. They buy in the morning, drive up the prices, and they sell before the day ends."

Brokers far removed from the trading floor say Smith is "uninformed." Compared to the stock market, they insist, the commodity exchange is "a goldfish bowl." It is much easier for a stock exchange floor specialist to finagle than for a commodity trader. But the Des Moines newspapermen found *bona fide* cases of rigging. And they quote a former high official of the Chicago Mercantile Exchange as saying that for every price rigging case prosecuted by the Commodity Exchange Authority (CEA), eight or nine are never discovered.

The CEA is the USDA agency responsible for regulating the futures markets, but according to the journalists the authority has largely relied on the professional traders to police themselves. Regulation, they said, actually declined in the years from 1965 to 1972, a period in which the volume of commodity trading zoomed from $65 billion a year to more than $200 billion.

Those caught in price manipulations receive little more than a slap on the wrist. A case cited is that of Cargill, Inc., which was found guilty of an illegal "squeeze" that pushed wheat futures up to artificial highs on the Chicago Board of Trade in 1963. The CEA took eight years to complete its case, say the Des Moines muckrakers, and then did not levy a fine or suspend Cargill's trading privileges; the authority merely imposed a meaningless two-year probation period.

A group of grain traders was alleged to have rigged

wheat futures on the Kansas City Board of Trade in 1972, which in some weeks handled a bigger volume of wheat trades than even the Chicago Board, in order to drive up the export subsidy. The CEA referred the charges to the Kansas City Board itself, and the board's investigation committees, made up of influential board members, including some Continental Grain Company officials, declared there was "no basis for complaint."

Not only newspapermen but also the inspector general of the Department of Agriculture and the General Accounting Office of Congress questioned whether complaints of market manipulations were being investigated promptly and vigorously enough. The CEA has a budget of less than $3 million and a staff of only 167; the Securities and Exchange Commission, which polices the stock exchanges, has a budget and staff more than ten times as large.

Told by the Office of Management and Budget to ask for no increase in its 1974 fiscal budget over fiscal 1973, CEA administrator Alex C. Caldwell complied. That brought criticism from an Iowa congressman, Republican Representative William J. Scherle. "You should have told OMB to go to hell. I don't feel in my own mind that the people of this country are adequately protected by your agency," said Scherle.

If wheat and soybean prices were manipulated in 1972, and nobody has proven they were, it is hard to say what effect, if any, the alleged rigging had on the feed grain prices farmers paid, or on the wheat prices paid by millers, exporters, and foreign countries. But the price of futures does affect the price of "actuals." When egg futures were allegedly manipulated in 1970, supermarket prices went up a dime a dozen, according to the head of the Department of Audits and Investigations at the Chicago Mercantile Exchange.

Chester W. Keltner, a Kansas City statistician who has written a book on commodity trading, reportedly stayed in the 1972 wheat market for almost the whole distance, missing only the final leg and going short at what he thought was the top. What Keltner (and the thousands who follow his weekly advisory service) missed from the peak, says gossip in the trade, he made up by profiting as the market went down. Keltner confirms the gossip.

But most buyers were in and out of the market many times on its way up; few had the nerve and patience to stick with it all the way. A wild gambler, pyramiding his buys with profits as the market climbed, might conceivably have run a mere $600 up to $50,000 in the booming 1972 wheat market. But for every winner there had to be a loser, so the high-rollers who cheered the Soviet wheat buys are balanced off by those who were threshed.

While hundreds of thousands of Americans speculated in commodity futures in 1972, some speculated more darkly on what the Soviet buying might mean.

Many saw apocalyptic overtones. Malthusian predictions of world famine, they suggested, might be coming closer to realization; despite the much acclaimed Green Revolution, the world might at last truly be on the brink of widespread starvation.

Rubbish, said some demographers. The world is perfectly capable of feeding itself if we can just solve the problems of food distribution. But there was no denying that agriculture, and thus the world's food supply, is still dependent on the vagaries of nature.

America's industrialized agribusiness has become so efficient that we are not only the world's largest food exporter but one of the few countries still in a position to export substantial tonnages of food staples. Yet America is not invulnerable to nature's caprices. When Belousov, Kalitenko, and Sakun came to buy American grain in July, 1972, many Eastern states were emerging from the ravages of Hurricane Agnes, later described by the U.S. Army Corps of Engineers as the worst natural disaster in the nation's history. Agnes wrecked hundreds of truck gardens and citrus groves. A corn blight, a wheat rust, an insect invasion, Mississippi floods, could still cripple American food production just as winterkill and drought sent Russia to the buying table in 1972.

Or is that really what made the U.S.S.R. buy so much grain in 1972?

In the opinion of some experts, the Russian purchase was motivated by more than simply a short crop. One reason the Russians bought so much wheat may be that they were able to buy it so cheaply. Another, that the Kremlin had made a basic decision to increase the level of Soviet livestock production.

But there are some suspicions that the Russian purchase was so large for reasons other than the U.S.S.R.'s own internal needs. Premier Aleksei N. Kosygin said that he was more concerned about China than about anything else, worried that China might take some rash action. During the India-Pakistan conflict, for example, there were fears that the Chinese might send troops to help Pakistan.

Russia and China both know from bitter experience how hard it is to fight a war on an empty stomach. Both nations suffered cruel food shortages during World War II. Is it possible that the Soviet Union was buying grain to keep it out of Chinese hands in anticipation of a possible confrontation with Peking, perhaps on the Indian subcontinent?

John Smith suggested that possibility to Morton Sosland in one of their telephone visits.

One can speculate endlessly, as one can about Mr. Smith himself.

Was he a commodity speculator? If he had bought futures contracts, he had no reason to publicize the Russian wheat purchases; the news was bound to come out soon enough, and he was bound to profit. But what if he were an undercapitalized speculator, trying to pyramid a small stake into a fortune? That would require faster action by the market, wouldn't it? It would. But without money, how could Smith have made all those transoceanic phone calls or gained such impeccable information?

Smith's knowledge of all the intimate details involved in the Russian buying mission's activities suggests an inside job. Were the Russians themselves speculating in futures? Or was the K. G. B. perhaps checking to see how good a job Belousov, Kalitenko, and Sakun were doing? Maybe Smith was working for Belousov, testing to make sure that the grain companies were following his demands that no news of the transactions be revealed.

By July 17, when Smith first phoned Sosland, Belousov had already bought over 7 million tons of U.S. wheat. Except for the relatively small amount he bought from Ned Cook on July 19, he had all the contracts he wanted. And he had bought his wheat at modest prices that later turned out to be a steal.

If the Russians wanted to make things difficult for the Chinese, now was the time to publicize the sales and push prices up, and watch the Chinese squirm as they tried to buy in a runaway market.

But if that was Smith's game, why did he phone on July 31 to say the Russians were back for more? And why did he sometimes inflate the amount of grain his putative comrades were buying?

Maybe Smith was a patriotic USDA employee who had access to C.I.A. information on Soviet crop failures, information the USDA had allegedly suppressed. That was the charge made in late October by Congressman Roman C. Pucinski, a Democrat from Illinois who was engaged in a losing campaign for the Senate seat of Charles Percy.

Senator George McGovern, after some internal party wrangling, had come out with a charge that the "cozy" relationship between the USDA and companies such as Continental, as illustrated by the job-jumping of men like Clarence Palmby, had somehow enabled the export companies to reap windfall profits. Pucinski implied that the profits had some connection with the information leaked to Sosland by Smith. Within a few days he called Sosland to apologize; he had been asked his views on the mysterious calls without having read Sosland's article revealing the Smith story in the October 3 issue of *Milling & Baking News*.

In fact, no scandal was ever substantiated; a Justice Department investigation found no criminal wrongdoing on the part either of a government employee, past or present, or of a grain company executive. Agriculture Secretary Butz, who was not exactly nonpartisan, called it "a clean bill of health."

But even as the Justice Department was submitting its report in early March, the comptroller general was testifying before the Senate Agriculture Committee. He criticized the "assurance given to exporters that they could, in effect, commit the U.S. government to make up the difference between an artificial target price and whatever prices domestic wheat might rise to without establishing a limit on quantities.

"The stage was thus set for the Russians to skillfully negotiate with individual exporters," said Elmer B. Staats. "The U.S. government, not a participant in the negotiations, nevertheless subsidized the transactions much beyond what appeared necessary or desirable."

To USDA protestations that it had no idea how much grain Exportkhleb was buying, Staats said the General Accounting Office believed "there were clear early signals from overseas and other sources concerning Russia's poor crop prospects and the dominant U.S. wheat supply situation."

Grumbling Texas and Oklahoma farmers vigorously seconded Staats's testimony that "farmers were not generally provided timely information with appropriate interpretive comments. Agriculture reports presented a distorted picture of market conditions."

That export companies received extraordinary profits from their sales to Moscow is hard to prove. Certainly most of what they received in subsidies went to defray the higher cost of the wheat they bought from terminal elevators, farmers' cooperatives, country elevators, and individual farmers. Some farmers went so far as to bring class actions against the export companies, against Clarence Palmby, and against the USDA.

The real surprise in the matter—and nothing could be more revealing of the change in American attitude toward the Communist powers in nine short years—is that the rancor of 1963 did not reappear. Even in an election year there were no angry debates in Congress, no early morning sessions, no "arm-twisting" by the President, no charges that selling wheat to Russia would be detrimental to the cause of freedom, no union boycotts.

As for Morton Sosland's informant, no USDA employee could have known so much about the travels and activities of the Belousov mission as Smith obviously knew. The theory does not wash; but there are always alternative theories.

Could Smith possibly have been working for the Chinese? This, too, has been suggested. China, like Russia, was having drought conditions in 1972. It, too, had poor grain crops. But for the Chinese, to come directly to America to buy grain as the Russians were doing would mean losing face.

Why would a country that wanted to buy wheat tell its operatives to leak information that would drive up wheat prices? But then, so goes the counterargument, China's only hope was to make the United States realize how much wheat the Russians were buying and to take action to limit the Russian purchase.

There was no public debate on the issue of selling grain to the Communists in 1972 because the sales were made in private. By the time the public got wind of them they were a *fait accompli*.

If no issues of political ideology were raised about the 1972 grain sales, the factors considered significant were possible hanky-panky, export subsidies, and farm subsidies. Not whether the sales might contribute to higher food costs for Americans.

As Nikolai Belousov and his confederates departed on their buying mission from Moscow at the end of June, 1972, a committee of fifteen young U.S. Department of Agriculture executives was putting the final touches on a study report urging an end to government price supports and farm subsidies.

The debate between subsidies and a free market economy was a perennial one in Congress: it would flare up again in 1973 when the Agricultural Act of 1970 expired. And the forty-three-page report of the USDA's committee would have an impact on that debate. It would also fuel some political speeches in the 1972 election campaigns.

A prime target of the report was the government definition of a farm as "a place of ten acres or more selling $50 worth of agricultural products a year," or a smaller place with sales of $250 or more, or even land whose owner had the "expectations" of satisfying these criteria.

Nonsense, said the committee headed by economist Allan S. Johnson. More than 80 percent of America's food production comes from less than a third of the nation's farms. The sales requirement should be raised to $5,000 a year. That would mean a total of less than 1.5 million U.S. farms, about half the 2.9 million total that could be classified as farms in 1970 by the old ten acres or $250 criteria.

Including smaller farmers, the committee said, "tends to exaggerate the low-income position of commercial farmers relative to the rest of the economy, and, hence, adds pressure" to raise farm commodity prices, although they may be already high enough for bigger farms to operate at a profit.

Parity, said the Johnson committee, should be junked and forgotten. It was no longer a sensible index of fair return to commodity producers. Direct federal payments to farmers, said the committee, should be "reduced to zero over a period of five years"; crop-support loan rates should be dropped to "disaster price" levels. Federal funds, said the committee, should be channeled toward creating new job opportunities for the people no longer needed on farms, not toward the efficient farms of modern agribusiness.

These were not new concepts. Don Paarlberg, the USDA's chief economist who denied any connection with the Johnson committee report, had written books making almost identical arguments. The American Farm Bureau Federation had taken the same position.

Overproduction, said critics of subsidy and price supports, was no longer a problem; it was time for America to stop living in the past.

The years since World War I, they pointed out, had seen a tremendous increase in farm productivity. Farms on the Great Plains that had earned $8 per acre in 1930 were now grossing as much as $100 per acre, and many farms ran to 1,000 acres and more. Taxpayers with incomes of $10,000 a year were helping to subsidize farmers with incomes as high as $100,000 a year. If farmers received 100 percent of parity, even a grossly inefficient farmer could live far better than the average farmer lived in the years between 1910 and 1914.

And instead of assuring the public of cheap food, it was charged, subsidies linked to output restrictions were having the opposite effect. Domestic food prices were going up because food production was not keeping pace with demand.

While domestic demand for food had been rising slowly, foreign demand was leaping ahead. And the buying of Exportkhleb in July and August, 1972, was giving the foreign demand for U.S. food commodities an unexpected and unprecedented upward push.

In an election year, the Johnson committee report

was a political hot potato. Former Agriculture Secretary Clifford Hardin had commissioned the study to review the "farm income question," but his successor, Earl Butz, reminded its authors that their conclusions ignored political realities. Copies of the report came with an attached statement by Assistant Secretary Richard Lyng saying the committee had "no official status" and that its views were not "representative of the policy of the Department."

Despite this disclaimer, the report raised a storm. Oren Lee Staley, president of the National Farmers Organization, called it "a blueprint for the elimination of farmers." The platform of the Democratic Party specifically repudiated the report, saying it "would eliminate the family-type farm . . . and put the farm people on the welfare rolls."

Some dispassionate observers insisted it would indeed be more sensible to give poor farmers welfare than to use a subsidy system that taxed consumers and increased their food costs to support prosperous farmers even more than poor ones.

There were, nevertheless, those political realities Earl Butz had mentioned. There was an election to win. As Morton Sosland's Mr. Smith had said, the Nixon administration was out to win favor with the farmers. "My mandate from the President," Earl Butz told an interviewer, "is to get farm incomes up."

Consumer advocates had been dismayed by the Butz appointment, partly because his record suggested he would be no great supporter of school lunch, school breakfast, and food stamp programs. His opponents recalled a speech in which Butz was supposed to have said, "There will always be a 'lower fifth' of our society. But let us not forget that the 'lower fifth' of our society today is better off than the 'upper fifth' in my day."

Even rank-and-file members of the American Farm Bureau Federation, the nation's largest and most conservative farm group, had protested the nomination, partly because Butz had served as assistant to President Eisenhower's unpopular agriculture secretary, Ezra Taft Benson, partly because he had been on the board of companies such as Ralston Purina, which refused to bargain with farmers, but mostly because Butz was considered a representative of big agribusiness.

The Butz nomination provoked a heated Senate hearing; it squeaked through by a narrow 51 to 44 vote.

Immediately on taking office, Butz began making good on his "mandate" to raise farm incomes. It is not the farmers who are responsible for rising food prices, he said; it is labor, middlemen, and consumers themselves who are bidding against each other for food. Farmers get only 38 cents of the food dollar, whereas the other 62 cents goes for processing, packaging, wholesaling, and retailing.

The new secretary paid lip service to the small farmer. "One of the problems that has been created in inner cities," he told an interviewer, "has been the exodus of rural people to downtown Baltimore, Philadelphia, Detroit, St. Louis, and New York, without the skills to be a productive citizen, without the cultural background to live there. They constitute a breeding ground for crime and delinquency, and cause welfare rolls to skyrocket. We should have kept them in the country. We could keep them much cheaper there, much more productive out there than we have them in the ghettos of the inner cities. There is a degree of social stability in rural America that you don't find in highly urban America."

But farming, said Butz, was "not a way of life, it's a way to make a living." There was nothing essentially good about a nation with a lot of small landowners "if they don't have enough land to make a decent living." This sounded like the Johnson committee report, which stated, "National policy should be directed toward maintaining agriculture as a viable industry and not as a way of life."

"One of my responsibilities," Butz said, "is to see that we have a continuing adequate food supply, and the best way to assure that is to let farmers make a little money in the process."

But if Butz had a mandate to "get farm income up," Chairman C. Jackson Grayson, Jr., of the Price Commission had a mandate to stabilize consumer prices. In mid-March, 1972, shortly before Butz flew to Russia, Grayson's irritation with Butz surfaced at a press conference. "The success of the President's program to stabilize prices requires that everyone work to hold prices down, not to push prices up, as Secretary Butz is advocating."

In the 1972 election, Earl Butz made the Nixon administration appear as the farmer's champion. And despite opposition from the National Farmers Union, the Agribusiness Accountability Project, and other critics who said Butz's policies would encourage vertical arrangements with giant food processors that would raise prices and lower quality, Butz was credited with saving the 1972 farm vote for the Republican Party.

Not until some weeks after the election did Earl Butz take any real action to hold down spiraling U.S. food prices or to encourage production of food that might be needed in hungry countries abroad.

10.

U.S. food prices were inching up in 1972 and soaring in 1973. Meat prices led the rise, but eggs, poultry, milk, and other foods were also getting more expensive. What kept prices from going even higher in most places was not so much price controls as a titanic supermarket price war, the biggest and most savage in the history of the $100 billion a year food industry.

The Great Atlantic & Pacific Tea Company, America's oldest supermarket chain and still the richest, had for years been losing money. While its competitors put up bigger stores in suburban shopping centers the A&P was late in vacating small, cluttered stores in poor urban areas. The chain's historic 10 percent share of the U.S. grocery market had declined to 6 percent. "The Tea Company," or "Grandma," as its employees called it, found itself for a twelve-month period from 1971 to 1972 in second place behind its archrival Safeway Stores, Inc., which had doubled its sales since 1962 while A&P sales remained static.

To reverse its staggering losses, the New York-based

A&P set out to win back customers. It launched a discount program that transformed all 4,200 A&P stores in thirty-five states, Canada, and the District of Columbia into "Warehouse Economy Outlets." The unwieldy slogan, "Where Economy Originates" (WEO) was used to promote wide-scale price-slashing that drove A&P competition to the wall. Competitive chains, especially in New York, Boston, Philadelphia, St. Louis, and Pittsburgh, had to cut their own prices, even though it meant operating at a loss and on borrowed money. Even the A&P, for the first time in its history, had to borrow money—$100 million. Some smaller chains were forced into bankruptcy.

Many stores emphasized non-food items like panty hose and toiletries on which they could make some profit; food stores returned almost to the old general store concept, although their fluorescent-lighted vastness lacked the reassurance of the old storekeeper's cracker barrel and Franklin stove.

Even in normal times, supermarkets sell many foods at a loss and average only about a penny and a half profit on every food sales dollar. Under Phase Two of the Economic Stabilization Program, retailers were unable to pass along increased labor, transportation, and other costs. And the price war trimmed their profit margins to less than 1 percent; many, in fact, operated at a loss.

While the price war lasted, U.S. consumers saved money on food. But it could not last indefinitely, and by the spring of 1973 it was ending. Even with so many retailers taking short markups, food prices had galloped ahead of all other retail prices and were threatening to wreck the Nixon administration's inflation control effort.

As suppliers raised prices, WEO stores and their competitors had to raise prices, too. The rises might be camouflaged by tricky two-for and three-for pricing (relatively few shoppers paid attention to unit prices in areas where they existed) but—here a penny or two, there a nickel or two—food prices were insidiously rising.

Meat is the major item on most Americans' shopping lists. It accounts for 25 to 30 percent of the average grocery bill. Almost all food prices were going up in 1972 and 1973, but the rapid rise in meat prices hurt the most.

A *New Yorker* magazine cartoon showed a butcher shop with a window sign reading, "Ask about our EAT NOW, PAY LATER plan."

Beef is the meat Americans prefer above all others. Nothing else comes even close. And even as beef prices rose, per-capita consumption of beef was rising. From 55 pounds a year in 1940, it climbed to 62 in 1952, to 89 in 1962, to 114 in 1970, and was projected for 1973 at 118, nearly half of it hamburger. (The average American eats, by comparison, only 73 pounds of pork, little more than 3 pounds of lamb, about 2.5 pounds of veal, over 40 pounds of poultry—a peculiar mix compared to European eating patterns, and an astonishing total alongside per capita figures for other countries.)

Much of the consumer wrath at supermarkets in 1972 and 1973 was directed at the high price of beef. But major food chains were selling beef as a loss leader to attract customers.

Dr. Earl Brown, a Cornell University business management professor with expertise in agriculture economics, told a *New York Times* writer that it was almost impossible to determine the net profits in the meat department of a food store at any one time.

"But if you could consider all the costs involved in meat operations you would find that the food chains are selling beef near the break-even point," he said.

Agriculture Secretary Earl Butz blamed rising meat prices on consumer affluence. Although beef production had more than doubled in twenty years (from 8.8 billion pounds in 1951 to 21.9 billion in 1971), it was still not keeping up with consumer demand. Personally, said Butz, he was happy beef prices were so high; it meant there were always plenty of the better cuts he preferred.

"Americans seem willing to pay higher prices," Butz complacently told a *U.S. News and World Report* writer. "As they get more purchasing power, they want to eat more beef."

There were statistics to show that beef was actually a bargain compared with other living costs. From 1952, at the peak of the Korean War, to 1972, beef prices had risen about 31 percent while the Consumer Price Index had risen about 56 percent, almost twice as much. But Americans were now eating almost twice as much beef, and they looked back yearningly at the 1952 price of 80 cents a pound for choice grade beef.

Importing more meat from abroad is often suggested as a way to increase supplies and thus lower prices, but under a 1964 law the amount of meat America imports can be limited by a quota program. In 1971, 600 million pounds of meat came from Australia, 250 million from New Zealand, 214 million from Mexico and Central America, 75 million from Ireland; a total of 1.24 billion pounds, about 7 percent of the meat America consumed, came from abroad. But early in 1972 a Rhode Island Democrat, Representative Fernand J. St. Germain, wrote President Nixon urging him to suspend quotas for the rest of the year "as a clear signal that the government is doing all it can to try to keep food prices somewhat in check."

In early June that request was echoed by a New York

Democrat, Representative Benjamin S. Rosenthal of Queens, who joined consumer advocates Betty Furness and Bess Myerson in a letter to the President that expressed "growing alarm over the relentless rise in the price of food, particularly beef."

Consumers, the letter charged, were being forced to pay "artificially high prices on certain major beef products because of the Administration's mistaken belief that import quota restrictions are necessary to protect the domestic cattle industry." The letter urged unrestricted beef imports.

But Nebraska Republican Senator Roman L. Hruska said the administration would face a fight from the prairies if it tried to force down meat prices by relaxing the import quota. The National Cattleman's Association raised a vociferous protest. And Earl Butz said housewives would not really benefit much from imported meat since most of it was used for hamburgers and frankfurters.

What the housewife wants, said the secretary, is "a nice choice roast or a good sirloin steak."

On June 26, 1972, President Nixon finally bowed to consumer pressure and removed meat quotas for the remainder of the year. Later he suspended quotas for 1973. The actions had little effect on meat prices. Most Australian and New Zealand beef and mutton had already been committed for export to other destinations. Ranchers in those down under countries were not about to increase their herds and flocks for the American market unless they could be assured of that market by permanent repeal of the 1964 meat quota law. A temporary suspension of quotas was not the same as a repeal in encouraging meat production for future years.

In any event, imported meat could not be expected to have any dramatic effect in lowering U.S. butcher shop prices. As long as prices remained high, there would be speculation as to possible reasons.

A House agriculture subcommittee in the summer of 1972 speculated that organized crime might be muscling in to push up meat prices by as much as 3 to 15 percent in some areas. New York City, which has the largest meat market in the country, was mentioned, and not without reason.

On July 27, while Nikolai Belousov in hot, muggy Moscow was learning the bad news about the Soviet drought, a New York Grand Jury was indicting officials of a wholesale meat supply house. Its president was charged with giving false and evasive answers to the jury that was investigating collusion among organized crime figures, corrupt labor union officials, and others to extort large sums of money from supermarkets. Many large chains in the metropolitan New York area, it was alleged, were selling meat at artificially high prices. The chains were threatened with labor strikes and meat supply cutoffs if they did not jack up prices and kick back some of the take to the mobsters.

During World War II days of black-market meat and stolen ration stamps, gangsters had infiltrated the meat business and some had never pulled out. New York's Merkel Meat company had been bought from the Merkel family by crooks who stuffed their frankfurters and other groundmeat products with tainted meat from cows, horses, and sheep that had died of disease. Another company was taken over by John Dioguardi, alias Johnny Dio, a reputed captain in the underworld family of the late Thomas Luchese. One of the men indicted by the grand jury in 1972 admitted to having close ties with Johnny Dio, who was serving a five-year stretch for bankruptcy fraud.

Most cattlemen, meat packers, and retailers are law-abiding businessmen. All disclaimed responsibility for the rapid rise in meat prices.

"Don't look at us," said cattlemen. They cited USDA Economic Research Service figures to show that their 64 cent share of the consumer's beef dollar was no higher than it had been in 1953, and while that share quickly climbed to over 70 cents, while only 43 cents of the overall food dollar (up from 38 cents) wound up in farmers' pockets, much of the cattlemen's gross went for feed.

Livestock production rises and falls with cattle, hog, and feed prices. In early 1971, farmers were faced with low hog prices and high feed prices (there had been a corn blight and bad weather in the Corn Belt). So farmers raised fewer hogs. In 1972, when prices for live hogs rose, production also rose, but only by 2 or 3 percent, because the price of feed was so high. Since it takes only five or six months to fatten a hog to 220-pound slaughter weight, a little more pork would be available by the fall of 1973 and that would take some of the pressure off prices.

Beef was more of a problem. In beef cattle, a cow's gestation period averages about nine months, and while a sow will have a litter a cow generally has just one calf. A rancher must wait nine months for a cow to produce a female animal; it may be two years before the heifer can be bred, another nine months before she calves, and at least sixteen months before her calf is ready for market. That adds up to more than four years. Any rancher who planned to expand his 1973 herd would first have to hold heifers back from market. And since heifers comprised almost half his calf crop, things would get worse before they got better.

U.S. beef cattle herds did increase by about 3 percent in 1972; cows for breeding accounted for more than half the increase, and a further increase in the breeding herd came in 1973. But USDA experts worried lest ranchers overproduce and create a beef glut by 1975. They projected a slaughter figure of 45.5 million head for that year, up from 37 million in 1973 and 39 million in 1974. That might sound good to hard-pressed consumers, who also applauded Washington's efforts to increase feed grain production. But the USDA, looking farther ahead, warned that higher cattle prices and lower feed prices might encourage ranchers to go overboard; yes, said the experts, beef prices would come down if ranchers raised more cattle, but if they raised too many and cattle prices dropped too low, the ranchers would then cut production; the shortages of 1973 would be repeated in 1976.

Consumers in 1973 had no patience for such long-range cautions. Prices of red meat were too high and something had to be done about it. Swift, Armour, Morrell, Wilson, and other meatpackers, large and small, were scrambling for cattle to keep their plants busy. They produced figures to absolve their industry of blame for the higher prices. Wholesale-retail markups of meat, the figures showed, had actually gone down a little from the 39 percent in 1967.

But in actual dollars, farmers were getting a lot more for their steers, packers were getting more for carcasses and primal cuts, retailers were getting fancy prices for ribs, briskets, shoulders, steaks, and hamburger. Wholesalers' margins, which went mostly to pay for breaking up carcasses, transporting them, refrigerating them, and delivering primal cuts to local stores, had gone up since 1967. So had retailers' margins, which went mostly to cover costs of cutting primal cuts into retail cuts, packaging them, and displaying them.

The carcass of a 1,000 pound choice grade steer was broken down by the packing house to 620 pounds of wholesale cuts, which were butchered by the wholesaler and retailer into 439 pounds of saleable beef. Ignoring the price differences from one cut of beef to another (and less than one-fifth of the meat is in club, porterhouse, sirloin, and T-bone steaks), a farmer or rancher at the end of 1972 who got 35 cents a pound for his beef on the hoof was receiving 70.1 cents a pound for the saleable beef on his animal. The meatpacker who slaughtered the animal received 80.8 cents; the wholesaler who delivered the primal cuts to retail stores received 84.6 cents; and almost $1.14 a pound went to the retailer whose back-room butchers cut the big sides and quarters of beef into retail cuts, trimmed the waste, packaged the cuts, displayed them in refrigerated cases, and rang up their prices at checkout counters.

Labor was the major cost item in all these operations. Individual backroom butchering is less efficient than centralized butchering, but low labor productivity at the retail level did not stop there; it ran through every phase of the supermarket industry.

Union men and their wives might complain of high meat prices, but union wage scales weighed heavily in the list of rising costs that were pushing up those prices. The costs kept retailers' profits on beef down to almost nothing, and in some cases to less than nothing.

Retail prices varied from one city to another; rump roast might be higher in Chicago than in Philadelphia, and round steak higher in Philadelphia than in Chicago. Prices also varied from one store to another in the same city. But in no city were they low enough to please hard-pressed housewives whose husbands liked meat with their potatoes.

If prices were to come down, cattlemen would obviously have to raise enough cattle to satisfy the demand at reasonable prices. Meanwhile, the only way to roll back prices seemed to be a reduction in that demand. In February, 1973, the chairman of the Federal Reserve Board told the Joint Economic Committee of Congress that it might be a good idea to revive the World War II idea of meatless Tuesdays. One meatless day a week, on a voluntary basis, might improve American diets while it helped bring down prices, said Arthur F. Burns. Let them eat cheese, he suggested.

World War II was in some other people's minds. When price controllers declined to clamp ceilings on raw agricultural commodities in early 1973, they argued such action would have negative results. It would decrease production by reducing incentive, and it would return the country to rationing and black markets.

George Meany, the seventy-eight-year-old president of the American Federation of Labor and the Congress of Industrial Organizations, disagreed. "There is only one way to control food prices," he told a news conference, "and that is to control them as we controlled them in World War II."

And what of the Russians? Were memories of bare wartime cupboards echoing in their heads when they came to America to buy all that grain in the summer of 1972? Or were they just determined to raise meat consumption in Russia to levels closer to those enjoyed by Americans? Anyway, how much did their buying have to do with the rise in U.S. meat prices?

Meat production is a business of converting plant protein—meaning grass, hay, and feed—into animal protein. After a calf is weaned at 250 to 400 pounds, 6 to 8 pounds of fodder and feed are needed to produce 1 pound of live weight, roughly 10 pounds of fodder and feed to yield a pound of meat. A steer will normally be range-fed until it weighs about 650 pounds (though the figure may vary from 500 to more than 850); it will then be "finished" in a feedlot to its slaughtering weight of about 1,000 pounds.

Meat prices may reflect losses of range animals in blizzards; they may go up in response to higher costs of farm credit, farm equipment, fertilizer, fuel, land, and labor, but the big cost item is feed. When feed prices go up, farmers are not generally eager to increase their livestock holdings, not even when live animals are fetching high prices. Too often the prices turn down, leaving profits too small to justify the high cost of feed.

In the spring of 1973, it was taking 26 to 28 cents worth of feed to produce a pound of beef; a year earlier it had taken only 20 cents worth. Soybean meal, the main source of protein in U.S. livestock feed, had more than doubled in price; beef finishers were switching from soybean meal to synthetic urea, which has no food value as such but nourishes animal rumen bacteria that produce protein from carbohydrates. Urea-fed animals needed more carbohydrates, and more carbohydrates meant more grain; wheat, an important feed grain, had gone up 57 percent, more than a dollar per bushel above its old price. Oats were up 17 percent. Even corn, America's largest crop by far and the predominant feed grain, was about 30 percent costlier than it had been a year earlier.

Some of these increases could be blamed on subsidy programs that kept croplands out of production. Some could be blamed on wet weather in large parts of the United States that had interfered with fall harvesting (and with planting of winter wheat in 1972 and with spring planting in 1973).

But even a marginal increase in demand can produce

a disproportionate, and disconcerting, leap in price. Demand for U.S. feed grains in 1973 was enlarged by two powerful factors; one was bad weather in the Midwest that caused cattle to burn up calories slogging through feedlot mud—it took more feed to produce the same amount of meat. The other factor was a swelling of export demand.

Demand for U.S. feed grains (often called meat-by-the-bushel) has been climbing for more than a dozen years as prosperous Europeans and Japanese ate more and more meat, poultry, eggs, and dairy products. American corn exports went from 210 million bushels in 1959 to 501 million in 1971; after the 1972 drought in so many countries they jumped to over a billion bushels—one-fifth the U.S. crop—in 1972–73. Soybean exports, only 141 million bushels in 1959, jumped to about 450 million in 1972–73 and would have gone higher had it not been for tariffs imposed by some countries to protect their less efficient farmers.

The 1973 figures for all feed exports, including wheat, were boosted by the extraordinary and unexpected purchases of Messrs. Belousov, Kalitenko, and Sakun. Their demand, piled atop the already high demand of the Japanese, the Dutch, the Italians, the West Germans, the Belgians, the French, and others, pushed feed grain and soybean prices to new heights.

Since feed represents up to 80 percent of a meat producer's cost the bulk of what farmers and ranchers were getting for their cattle, hogs, and lambs in 1973 was going to pay the higher cost of feed. And when the price of bacon, spareribs, veal cutlets, porterhouse, and sirloin went out of sight, it was mostly because feed grain prices had gone out of sight.

High feed grain prices made lawmakers reluctant to end completely the use of DES, the synthetic sex hormone employed since the 1950s to help cattle gain more weight on less feed. By 1972, nearly 90 percent of all U.S. beef cattle was being finished on feed containing DES, but on August 1, the day Exportkhleb bought nearly 3 million tons of U.S. wheat on its return visit to New York, the FDA had announced a ban on the use of DES in livestock feed rations.

A small number of women, whose mothers had received therapeutic doses of the hormone in pregnancy to avoid miscarriage, had in their late teens or early twenties developed cancer of the vagina; so while DES was sometimes prescribed with FDA approval as an emergency morning-after contraceptive measure, traces of DES in meat were considered potentially carcinogenic. Such traces were occasionally found in meat from animals whose rations had contained DES, so the FDA was required by law to prohibit the use of DES in feed. The ban took effect January 1, 1973; ear implants of DES, probably less effective but much less likely to leave traces, were still permitted. Since it would take 500 pounds more grain to fatten beef for slaughter if use of the hormone were totally eliminated, the FDA estimated that a ban would raise beef prices by $3\frac{1}{2}$ cents a pound. That estimate was made before feed grains jumped to their new plateaus; the complete ban on DES announced by the FDA in April, 1973, would add at least 6 cents a pound to beef prices. It would require use of an additional 3 million tons of grain.

To control red meat prices without controlling feed grain prices seemed a questionable course, and as late as March 20, 1973, Earl Butz was holding out against any meat price controls, though he admitted "some damned fools in the administration disagree with me."

George Meany was threatening huge wage increase demands unless something was done about food prices, and on March 29 the "damned fools" had their way: Richard Nixon decreed on television that retail prices of beef, lamb, mutton, pork, and veal would be allowed to go no higher than their peak prices of the previous thirty days. The ceilings were called "temporary"; they would be removed, officials predicted, before black marketeers had time to get organized.

Treasury Secretary Shultz called the ceilings a form of "rationing." He said, "I think the sellers, with their prices at a ceiling, obviously will not be able to buy at prices that are going to have them lose money. In effect, this restriction on demand, buttressing the restrictions that the housewife herself is placing on it, tends to be passed back down the distribution pipeline."

Nobody was much pleased by the ceilings. Some food industry sources called them a "simplistic" attack on the problem. George Meany, saying "the damage already is done," pressed for more effective controls, including mandatory price reductions. Consumers echoed the cry for rollbacks; many staged boycotts at supermarkets. People tried meat "analogs" made of soy protein. They ate more cheese, macaroni, peanut butter, and tuna. Suddenly it became popular to observe Lent. Even after Easter.

"I don't think the boycott activity of these activists amounts to a mammary gland on a mudworm" said the president of the National Association of Food Chains as the boycott began on April Fool's Day. Clarence Adamy pointed out that consumers had begun resisting higher prices six weeks earlier, not as a demonstration of protest but simply because they balked at paying outrageous prices. Briefer but more intense than the general super-market boycotts of 1966 and 1969 (which sensibly de-manded an end to promotional store games and trading stamps, as well as protesting high prices), the 1973 meat boycott allowed suburbanites and other more affluent Americans to vent their wrath at inflation. Taking it out on meat had little immediate effect on prices; farmers merely withheld animals from market (though a delay of more than ten days or so was uneconomic), meatpackers laid off thousands of workers. If anything, the boycott dampened any enthusiasm on the part of cattlemen and farmers to breed more livestock, thus assuring a continua-tion of inadequate meat supply.

Fish and poultry, which had no ceilings, became more expensive. Retailers in many cases marked up prices of nonmeat items to offset losses on red meat. Butchers trimmed off less fat and bone (profit margins in meat are measured in fractions of ounces, and although scales can be checked, some more subtle forms of chiseling are virtually impossible to police).

"I don't want to decrease demand," said Earl Butz. "Our job is to increase output." But demand did decrease as prices rose, and prospects for increased meat supplies were scarcely brightened by price ceilings on retail meat. Unless Americans changed their eating habits radically and permanently, and unless feed prices came down, the outlook for a return to 1972 prices on hamburger, lamb chops, sirloin, and spareribs was exceedingly dim.

Russians might be increasing their meat consump-tion; many Americans would be eating less meat. And complaining about it. Few would accept the fact that most Americans eat too much meat, that many would improve their nutritional health by eating more fish and poultry,

more bread, more fruits and vegetables, and less food
altogether.

Not everyone can eat as high off the hog as Earl Butz,
who spends less than 10 percent of his after-tax income on
food.

For less affluent Americans food often takes half a
family's income, and for many Americans, as for most of
the world, meat is a luxury.

Bread is the everyday staple—white, enriched, pre-
sliced, and prewrapped. In 1972 more bread was sold in
one and one-half pound loaves than in the traditional one
pound loaves in U.S. supermarkets. And because of the
hard-fought supermarket price war, bread prices were
lower on average in October than they had been in May.
But bakers could not absorb their higher costs forever.

One-third of the $6 billion U.S. bakery business is
in the hands of six gigantic companies—ITT-Continental
(no kin to Continental Grain), Interstate Brands, Camp-
bell-Taggart, American, General, and Ward; about $3.25
billion of the bakery business is shared by 350–400 independent bakeries, and the remaining $750 million is done
by captive bakeries maintained by retail chains like A&P,
Safeway, and Jewel.

A wholesale baker in Wisconsin complained during
the spring of 1973 that his white flour had gone up 31.4
percent in price, higher than the increase in his lard (30.1
percent), his salt (11.4 percent), his yeast (6.6 percent),
his sweetener (3.1 percent), and his labor (7 percent). Flour
had gone up as wheat prices climbed.

"I'm desperate," the baker said.

According to the Independent Bakers Association,
more than forty independent bakeries went out of business
in the eight months beginning July, 1972, and although

some of these were merged into other bakeries, more than 5,500 people lost their jobs.

The Cost of Living Council had approved a 1.5 to 2 percent increase in the price of a pound loaf of bread late in 1972, but that did not cover all the higher costs of bread-making. And whatever the council said, it was the Big Six who determined the prices of bread, hamburger and hot dog buns, biscuits, rolls, cakes, and the like in their markets.

The prices of all those items would inevitably go up. At 24.5 cents a one-pound loaf, the average price of white bread in 1972, bread was 81 percent costlier than it had been at its old 1947–49 price of 13.5 cents. Farmers, bakers, middlemen, and retailers, however, sliced the 24.5 cents loaf differently from the way they had sliced the old 13.5 cent loaf.

The farmer got only 3.5 cents, just 6 percent more than the 3.3 cents he had received a quarter-century earlier. The miller's share was .6 cents, exactly his old share. The baker got 14 cents, 122 percent above his old 6.3-cent share (but his after-tax profit was only 2.3 percent of sales, down from 2.6 percent five years earlier). Transportation and storage costs ate up 1.8 cents, 64 percent above the old 1.1-cent figure. The retailer got 4.6 cents, 109 percent above his old 2.2 cent share (but his after-tax profit, too, was lower).

In March, 1973, a Republican senator from Texas, John Tower, proposed an amendment to the wage-and-price-control authority that would have permitted a 3 cent rise in the price of bread because "200 independent bakers today are operating in the red." The bakers, said Tower, were unable to raise prices to reflect their higher flour costs. A Connecticut Republican, Senator Lowell P. Weicker, Jr., called the Tower proposal a "bread tax," and the Senate voted it down 53 to 26. The Cost of Living Council nevertheless permitted some major bakers to raise prices by as much as 8.31 percent at the end of March.

Many bakers were being hurt by higher flour costs, but much of the price of bread had little to do with the price of flour. While Russians complained of a lack of variety in the wares available to them, U.S. consumers were plagued with a costly excess of variety. A bakery truck driver-salesman going into a supermarket often had to deliver more than two dozen different kinds of bread —butter bread, buttermilk bread, cheese bread, cinnamon raisin bread, diet bread, egg bread, potato bread, raisin bread, sandwich bread, sprouted wheat bread, stone ground whole wheat bread, and every other bread Madison Avenue or the health food industry could promote. The special breads invariably cost far more than their ingredients warranted.

Special or ordinary, each loaf had a code date on its wrapper, often with a colored twister to help the driver-salesman pick up stale bread. A loaf of bread has a shelf life of about forty-eight hours. With so many different kinds of loaves on store shelves, returns of stale bread were bound to increase.

Often six or more baker-wholesalers delivered to a store each day. Driver-salesmen often placed the bread on store shelves themselves, and although bakers liked having their own men do that job to get a better competitive position and more shelf display, it was a job supermarket stockclerks could handle more economically. According to the USDA, a $300 a week driver-salesman in 1972 could deliver on his $2,000 route only about two-thirds as much as he had delivered twenty years before, even if he was now a younger man. Americans were paying for these distribution inefficiencies, including the proliferation of bread varieties. Abridging choice is abridging freedom, but the freedom of having more than two dozen different kinds of bread, plus additional dozens of bun, roll, cake, cookie, and pastry varieties, can be expensive.

Some retailers sold bread for as much as 10 cents less than advertised brands, and day-old bread often went at a further discount. The lower-priced bread, labeled with store names, was baked either in the stores' own bakeries or by wholesale bakers who also had advertised brands. But as advertised brands went up in price, so generally did stores' private-label breads. Somebody had to pay for the higher cost of wheat that raised the cost of flour that forced bakers to hike prices and increased the take of driver-salesmen.

Russians in 1973 often had to queue up for their daily bread, but they still bought it at the same price as the year before. Not only U.S. taxpayers, but the poor of America, its big bread eaters, were subsidizing Russian housewives.

So, in effect, were the people of China, India, Bangladesh, and Japan, of all the countries that import wheat, and that paid through the nose for wheat when Soviet buying forced up prices.

11.

In 1966 two brothers, Paul and William Paddock, published a book predicting worldwide famine by the year 1975. The most immediate candidate for famine was India, which was saved in 1966 and 1967 only by millions of tons of donated U.S. wheat.

America had plenty of wheat. Its farmers were encouraged to plant less of it; U.S. taxpayers complained about the high cost of storing surpluses. But after the shipments to India, surplus stocks were sharply reduced, as they were again after the shipments to Russia in 1972 and 1973.

Still, not many people took the Paddock brothers very seriously. Hardy semidwarf varieties of wheat, developed in Mexico by Rockefeller Foundation scientists, were yielding as much as fifty bushels per acre on land in India that had once yielded only ten.

At the International Rice Research Institute in the Philippines, and at the Aduthurai experimental station in Madras, India, researchers funded by Ford and Rockefeller Foundation grants had developed new rice varieties.

One third of all the world's rice lands are in India, and the new varieties yielded thousands of pounds per acre, where India's average had been only 600 (although it took an abundance of fertilizer and water to make the miracle seeds perform their magic, and only farmers able to obtain credit could afford the necessary outlays for seed, fertilizer, and irrigation).

Prime Minister Indira Gandhi said India's Green Revolution was eliminating the need for any continuing food imports. Her country was finally achieving its goal of self-sufficiency. But while food production was indeed increasing so was India's population. Despite a frenzied effort to stem the birth rate, with wide distribution of free contraceptive devices, mostly condoms, and a well-publicized program of incentives to encourage vasectomies, India's 560-million population was headed toward the billion mark by the end of the century.

Even as Mrs. Gandhi spoke, drought was cutting into Indian food production. In the northwest, where rainfall averages twenty to thirty inches a year, only ten inches fell in 1971, and only eight in 1972. Throughout India's central states, monsoon rains came late. Bihar, where hundreds of people had starved to death in 1967, and Rajasthan were especially parched, but there was drought in thirteen of India's twenty-one states, from Bengal to Maharashtra. Some 50 million people live in Maharashtra, which lost about 70 percent of its crop.

With nearly 30 million more people to feed than in 1971, the country had less grain with which to feed them. To keep food production gains from being canceled by population growth, India needed irrigation. Beneath the land lay vast reservoirs of water. But all of India, the world's largest democracy, produces no more electricity than is needed to run the city of New York. Enormous progress has been made in the twenty-five years since India broke loose from the British Empire; only 1 percent of her rural villages were electrified then whereas today more than 20 percent of the 560,000 villages have electric power. Still, there is nowhere near the amount of power necessary to operate tube wells that could tap India's underground water resources for irrigation. And in 1972 and early 1973, low water levels in the nation's rivers combined with troubles in coal transit to cut into India's already pitifully low energy output. The ambitious rural electrification program ground to a halt.

Cattle are the main source of power in rural India and cattle ownership has long been a measure of a man's wealth. But in 1973 beasts were considered a burden. A story was told that a cow was sold for a bunch of bananas. A farmer reportedly touched the feet of a truckdriver in gratitude after the driver accidentally killed his famished water buffalo. Used by Hindus only for milk and power, the cattle roamed the countryside, devouring crops, stripping the leaves off trees, eating anything they could find, and dying in droves for lack of fodder.

Indian grain traders, anticipating further scarcities, hoarded grain, which sent prices up 20 to 30 percent. There were reports of people surviving on the flowers of mahua trees, which sprout during the dry seasons. Refugees by the thousands sought food and water in camps set up outside Bombay, a city already bloated with hungry Indians.

Only in late November and December did rains come to end the drought. In nearly half of Bihar and Uttar Pradesh, in much of Rajasthan and West Bengal, in Gujarat, in most of Madhya Pradesh and Haryana, the rainfall was too little and too late. Officials of the Church World Service, a large U.S. voluntary relief agency, predicted the worst famine conditions of the twentieth century. Maharashtra, said the CWS in January, was experiencing its "worst famine in living memory." Rajasthan was having famine "the like of which it has never known before."

In some states food riots seemed imminent. At a news conference in New Delhi, India's Food Minister Fakhruddin Ali Ahmed said a third of the people, 200 million, were affected by drought.

Ahmed estimated that India's food grain production for the year ending June 30, 1972, had been only 100 million tons, 15 million below the goal initially set, 4 million below the harvest of the previous year, 8 million below the year before that. It was India's worst harvest since 1968. Government grain stocks amassed during the six previous years had dropped from 9.5 million tons to only 2.5 million by fall harvest time, and the harvest had replenished stocks by only a million tons.

With her population growing by more than a million people each month, India's food needs were now becoming serious, if not desperate. Little buffer against starvation remained in the state warehouse.

A year before Mrs. Gandhi had canceled an order for 400,000 tons of U.S. grain and had said there would be no further grain imports. Now Indians bewailed her haughty termination of the country's fifteen-year-old Food for Peace Agreement with the United States. Under that agreement, New Delhi could buy U.S. grain with rupees; the sellers were reimbursed by the U.S. government in hard currency.

To keep her grain shops open, to keep people from rioting, India was forced in January, 1973, to contract for 2 million tons of grain, more than half of it from the United States, the rest from Canada and Argentina. She was obliged to pay in hard currency, not rupees. And the price—driven up by Soviet purchases—was far higher than the $60 to $65 a ton paid by the Russians.

To buy 1.5 million tons of wheat at $110 a ton, plus half a million tons of grain sorghum at $70 a ton (including $15 a ton for shipping), India had to pay about $200 million, some of it in Canadian dollars and Argentine pesos. This was nearly a fifth of the nation's hard currency reserves, which India desperately needed for irrigation projects in areas where drought was more probable than a good monsoon. To spend the money on stopgap food supplies was to put off the possibility of avoiding hunger in those areas for years to come.

There were reports that the 2 million tons of grain bought in January, 1973, represented only a fifth of what India might need, though rains that month and in March improved the outlook for India's own crop. If New Delhi had bought the wheat in August and September, 1972, when it first knew the country was in trouble, $200 million would have bought nearly 3 million tons instead of just 2 million; Prime Minister Gandhi had resisted buying partly out of pride, partly because her bureaucracy is never more than dimly aware of what is happening with regard to India's irrigation projects, her allocation of high-yielding seeds, her distribution of fertilizer, or her harvest yields.

At the end of February, critics in the Indian Parliament expressed fears that Mrs. Gandhi's government might fail to avert famine. The drought, she replied, had caused losses only in coarse grains, not in wheat or rice. The Green Revolution had not failed. Prices had gone up by as much as 13 percent because "vested interests," meaning traders, had hoarded supplies to create a "psychology of scarcity." Beginning March 15, the government Food Corporation of India took over the wholesale grain trade except for "marginal imports."

While the drought had been of "unusual magnitude," the problem was "not insurmountable." Mrs. Gandhi said, "We have no intention of failing. We're going to succeed. We shall overcome." But she admitted that she had not foreseen the large-scale drought when she spoke in 1971 of achieving self-sufficiency in food. And when grain prices boiled up after nationalization, and an estimated 2.5 million were put out of work, she admitted that nationalizing the grain trade might not work.

What had turned Mrs. Gandhi against U.S. Food for Peace aid was America's support of Pakistan during the 1971 conflict over East Bengal, now Bangladesh. The U.S.S.R. had supported India in that short-lived confrontation, China and the United States had sided with Pakistan. And when Pakistan was pinched for grain in the early months of 1973, and had to import nearly a million and a half tons of wheat, most of it was U.S. wheat brought in under the Food for Peace program.

In the Punjab, Pakistan's fertile breadbasket that is home for 63 percent of the nation's 50 million people, the wheat is harvested in April and May. Food prices always climb during the three months prior to harvest. In January, at the start of the hungry season, food prices were already steep in Pakistan, although in India and Afghanistan they were even higher. Pakistan's President Zulfikar Ali Bhutto's provincial food minister in Lahore was not optimistic about keeping prices down even to the high January levels. Pakistan subsequently got rain and harvested a record wheat crop of nearly 8 million tons, but food was short before the harvest. One reason for the shortage, according to President Bhutto, was that 100,000 tons of Pakistani wheat had been smuggled across the border to Afghanistan.

In Peshawar, capital of Pakistan's North-West frontier province, the right-wing Jamaat-i-Islam Party demonstrated against high food prices. The government in Sind was forced by protests to cancel its three-day-old sweetless day program, designed to conserve sugar. Pakistan theoretically grows enough sugar for her domestic needs, but in 1969 Field Marshal Mohammed Ayub Khan had been forced out of the presidency by riots over sugar shortages, and Bhutto, remembering Ayub Khan's 1964 prediction that "in ten years' time, human beings will eat human beings in Pakistan," was clearly apprehensive. With its big wheat harvest, and its imports from America, Pakistan was able to export rice, whose world price had doubled, and earn foreign exchange for sugar imports, but the country's fortunes were still in the hands of fickle weather.

Like housewives with overextended food budgets, some governments in 1973 were at their wits' end trying to keep their citizens fed and content.

For countries such as Pakistan and India, where wheat is used to make chapati, the flat bread food staple, the world shortage of wheat meant special hardship. With U.S. reserves so diminished, relief agencies worried that short supplies, high prices, and shipping bottlenecks might jeopardize their programs for supplying food aid, not only to Pakistan but to Colombia, Turkey, and other hard-pressed countries that rely on Food for Peace wheat.

For years this wheat has been distributed in sacks marked, "From the people of the United States," as if the knowledge that they were accepting charity would make hungry people love their benefactors. Little charity is involved. World hunger is a threat to American security, and averting that hunger is more than just humanitarian: it is a matter of enlightened self-interest.

It is also a matter of commercial self-interest. The main emphasis of the 1954 law (Public Law 480) was never on helping the economic development of recipient countries in the first place; it was on disposing of U.S. surpluses whose producers had no market and were threatened with falling prices. Only commodities in surplus could be shipped under P.L. 480. So while butter, cheese, dry skim milk, and vegetable oils were donated, or sold for native currency (funny money, it was called), in the earlier years of the program, as U.S. stocks of those foods declined in the 1960s almost the only remaining Food for Peace was wheat.

And in 1972 and 1973 wheat had ceased to be a surplus commodity.

Before harvesting began in the spring of 1972, America had carry-over wheat stocks of almost 24 million tons from previous harvest years. Domestic U.S. consumption of wheat for food is 14 million tons, so even if 10 million went for seed and feed, the nation still had a comfortable cushion.

But after selling close to 33 million tons to the Soviet Union and other countries, America's carry-over reserve by early 1973 was little more than 10 million tons, less than half what it had been the year before, well below the 17 million ton average for 1965 to 1969.

It was the lowest figure since the 1950s. And not all the wheat in reserve was of the kinds most suitable for use in baking bread; of those kinds there would be barely enough to protect Americans from a bad 1973 harvest. As it was, hard winter wheat was in short supply and bakers needed flour from that relatively low-protein wheat to mix with higher protein wheat flour in order to get dough that had desirable baking characteristics.

A USDA official said in November, 1972, that U.S. wheat reserves were in no danger of dropping to the low level of 1967, when shipments to India had so depleted them. In fact, they dropped below that level. And Washington seemed about to cut the amount of wheat it would give away. There were reports that the USDA was proposing a 50 percent slash in total funds ($1 billion in 1972) appropriated under P.L. 480, but spending remained at close to earlier levels.

Some people who had scoffed at the Paddock brothers' alarmist predictions in 1966 were now less quick to dismiss those doomsday famine predictions.

12.

Orientals eat rice. Everybody knows that. Rice is the principal food staple for half the human race. What most people do not realize is that Orientals are also big consumers of wheat. The biggest cash customer for U.S. wheat for years has been Japan. And for almost every bushel of soft white wheat that Japan buys for noodles, it buys a bushel of hard spring or winter wheat for bread.

Until shipwrecked Portuguese sailors introduced bread into Japan in 1543, no Japanese had ever tasted bread. Many Japanese got their first taste only after World War II, four centuries later, when large quantities of U.S. wheat were shipped into Japan, whose own native wheat is better suited to noodle-making. Instant noodles (*sokuseki ramen*) burgeoned into a Japanese staple in the 1950s and 1960s, and so did bread.

In world trade, wheat is much cheaper than rice. Even in 1972, when the world price of wheat rose from $60 a ton to $100, it did not approach the $165 a ton level of rice. For a country to eat more wheat and less rice can make good economic sense, and the Japanese were quick to realize that fact.

After World War II, in which Japan was aborted in its "co-prosperity sphere" effort to aggrandize the small home island croplands with acquisitions in Manchuria and Indochina, the Japanese embarked on a peaceable new course to keep their people well fed. They legalized abortion to control the number of mouths to feed. More important, they made a calculated decision, straight out of Adam Smith's *Wealth of Nations,* on which Japan's big and growing consumption of wheat flour today is essentially based: like imperialist powers of ages past, Japan would obtain cheap raw materials—including food —from abroad, while at home it would concentrate its energies and capital on making steel, automobiles, cameras, textiles, and other industrial goods.

Within a quarter-century, Japan was exporting so many TV sets, bicycles, calculators, baseball gloves, transistor radios, tape recorders, and even American flags to America that Japan's imports from the United States, however large, still left a tremendous trade surplus. In 1971 the United States suffered its first trade deficit in the twentieth century, and despite a devaluation of the dollar (taking into account upward valuations of foreign currency, it amounted to about 12 percent) in December of that year, the $2 billion 1971 deficit grew in 1972 to $6.3 billion. The world's greatest industrial power was importing more than it was exporting.

More than half of the U.S. trade deficit came from trade with Japan, a country which was exporting more than it was importing. A major source of Japan's raw materials, ironically, was America, whose most efficient, most competitive industry was agriculture.

Persuading Japanese consumers to switch from costly rice to cheaper wheat had not been easy. Tokyo had done it with a massive school lunch program, more ambitious—

and more effective—than anything ever attempted in the United States. Children learned early to enjoy bread and rolls, and they grew up liking bakery products. Soon big baking companies were developing brand names and turning out millions of loaves in dozens of varieties to meet the evolving demand. Bakery shops sprang up that sold nothing but bread and cakes. Sandwich shops opened next door to traditional *sushi* shops. Some bakeries went into doughnut making; the obligatory gift one Japanese businessman gives another became in some cases a box of doughnuts.

Japan still ate nearly three times more rice than wheat products, but rice consumption was steadily declining and wheat consumption was going up. And since it cost nearly three times as much to grow a bushel of wheat in Japan as in America, more than 80 percent of Japan's wheat came from abroad.

Consumption of eggs, meat, milk, and poultry has risen sharply in Japan since World War II, contributing to the growing body-size of Japanese people, but the Japanese still average little more than 5 pounds of beef per year (beef prices are three to six times the highest U.S. levels), 11 pounds of pork, and 9.5 pounds of poultry; a big and seldom mentioned part of the postwar Japanese dietary revolution has been an increasing use of bread.

At the same time that it was subsidizing Japanese rice farmers, Japan's Food Agency was buying about 5 million tons of wheat a year at world prices and selling it to millers at much higher prices (although some was used for feed). This price-spread normally enabled the Food Agency to make a substantial contribution to Japan's national budget, but in 1972 the world price of wheat was pushed up a dollar a bushel by Soviet buying. The Food Agency could not make its usual high profit.

An effort was made to keep America's best dollar customer for wheat well supplied, but smart, sophisticated Japanese trading companies such as Mitsui and Mitsubishi, accustomed to ordering a specific quality of wheat for delivery on a specific date at Kobe, Tokyo, or Yokohama, were obliged to accept any wheat they could get.

In other parts of Asia, too, the use of wheat flour has been rising, although to many Orientals flour is still as strange a food as squid or poi is to most Americans. Nevertheless, South Korea, Taiwan, the Philippines, and other Asian customers have been importing some 4 million tons of wheat each year. Together with Japan, they have accounted for about 30 percent of U.S. wheat exports. (Some of the wheat they take is bulgur, developed for countries accustomed to boiling rice; but most rice eaters are not easily switched.)

All of these Asian nations are dwarfed by the People's Republic of China, hostile neighbor to the U.S.S.R., feared by Russians since the days of Genghis Khan's Mongol hordes, exploited by the Russians in the days of the Czars, resentful of the Soviets for not making good on Lenin's 1920 pledge to return "gratis and forever everything the Czarist regime and the Russian bourgeoisie rapaciously stole" from China.

To what extent was the massive buying of grain by the Soviets in 1972 influenced by the simmering rivalry between the two great Communist states?

Like Russia, China has a long history of food shortages. Some part of China has experienced famine every year for two millennia; natural disasters such as drought and flood are only part of the reason for China's chronic hunger.

Confucius, in the fifth century B.C., encouraged

large families with no rule of primogeniture; this meant a farmer's lands were divided among his sons, and the sons' lands among *their* sons, with agricultural units growing progressively smaller, and less productive, at each division.

Unlike Europe and America, China had few urban factories to draw off surplus rural labor; population pressures on available farmland increased generation after generation. In Europe and America, intellectuals took an interest in problems of agriculture, but in China men of letters disdained practical matters and contributed nothing to boosting farm output. The Physiocrats of Louis XV's France; Holland's Jan Ingenhousz; France's Antoine Lavoisier; Germany's Justus von Liebig; America's Washington, Franklin, and Jefferson; England's Priestley, Gilbert, and Lawes had no counterparts in eighteenth- or nineteenth-century China.

What China had was manpower. Beginning in 1949, when Mao Tse-tung, Liu Shao-ch'i, and their comrades proclaimed the People's Republic in Peking, the Communists began to mobilize that manpower. By 1952 they had set up an equitable system for distributing available food.

But in the first Five-Year Plan that followed, production of cereal grains such as rice and wheat failed year after year to meet targets set by Peking. Chinese industry performed brilliantly, producing record tonnages of iron, coal, cement, and steel, but in the spring of 1955 Peking warned that "if growth of agricultural production does not catch up, it is bound to affect . . . the speed of industrialization."

Where European Marxists had predicated their philosophies on an industrial proletariat, Mao had been supported by a rural proletariat, attracted to his cause in some provinces by the scorched-earth tactics of the invading Japanese in the 1930s and '40s. China's future as a Communist state, Mao maintained, lay in mobilizing the peasants. But whereas Mao insisted that "collectivization must precede mechanization," Liu Shao-ch'i called for the opposite order of priorities; following Marxist orthodoxy, he said large farms needed chemical fertilizers, electrification, tractors and other machinery, plus skilled agronomists, engineers, and economists.

Through most of the first Five-Year Plan, Liu prevailed. Little of China's development budget went to the rural sector; so while coal and cement output doubled, and the production of iron and steel increased more than fourfold, Chinese peasants, some of them working in loose cooperatives but still not collectivized, lacked seed, chemical fertilizers, farm tools, adequate draft animals, and credit. Unable to pay their debts, many poor peasants were forced to sell their land and become laborers.

To counter the rising trend toward rural capitalism, in July, 1955, Mao proposed the rapid enlargement of cooperatives into giant collective farms. Senior Party leaders such as Liu opposed Mao; they recalled the awful turmoil in Russia twenty years earlier when Stalin's first Five Year Plan had shipped kulaks to Siberia and had wrecked Soviet agriculture. Less ambitious collectivist efforts a year or two earlier in China had got the peasants' backs up; farm output had dropped.

But this time Mao prevailed; and the Russian story of the early 1930s was repeated in 1956 China. By the end of that year, about 100 million peasant families were incorporated in big collective farms called Agricultural Producers' Cooperatives.

Agricultural harvests in China during 1956–57 fell to levels well below the rate of population increase, partly for reasons of weather but also because many peasants rebelled at the prospect of becoming tenants of the state. Rather than surrender their livestock and draft animals to the collective, they slaughtered them. They destroyed their farm implements. They neglected their confiscated fields.

Famine broke out in Kwangsi province and probably elsewhere. Some collectives disbanded, peasants poured into the cities, food supply systems were strained.

Surviving a brief power struggle, Mao purged dissident Party officials in rural China and by late 1957 had launched a still more ambitious effort to mobilize the peasantry. This was The Great Leap Forward, which in less than a year put more than half a billion peasants into 26,000 "people's communes."

Deprived of all private property, the peasants were organized into labor brigades. They were guaranteed food, clothing, shelter, child care, everything to everybody "according to his needs." But as they were shifted from field to makeshift steel furnace to dam construction site in a frenzy of forced labor, the peasants were diverted from their spring planting. That work was undertaken in part by office workers, students, and factory hands, who were taken from the overcrowded cities and shipped off to rural villages.

Caught up in the dynamism of The Great Leap Forward, skeptics such as Premier Chou En-lai and Liu Shao-ch'i publicly endorsed Mao's program. The excitement and genuine enthusiasm of the populace is illustrated by the organized demonic energy that went into purging the country of the "four pests": flies, mosquitoes, rats, and sparrows. (Bedbugs were substituted for sparrows when the disappearance of the birds disrupted the ecology and set off a caterpillar boom.)

The Great Leap Forward demonstrated the potential of people power, but in the end it was a dismal failure. Because of mismanagement, dikes and irrigation ditches were neglected with resultant flooding. Energies were futilely dissipated in makeshift "backyard furnaces" that produced poor quality iron and steel if any at all. Mao's "eight principles" of agriculture, which included plowing furrows as much as six feet deep and planting rice seedlings one to two inches apart, led to crop failures. The soil was ruined in some areas by misguided irrigation and dam projects.

Exhausted by overwork, malnourished because of food shortages, millions of Chinese fell sick. Grain output in 1960 dropped to 150 million tons, less than it had been in 1952 when there were 100 million fewer Chinese to feed. Through strict rationing, the staggering death tolls of earlier famines were avoided, but in Kansu province as many as 70,000 reportedly died of starvation. A French correspondent in Peking was reminded of "the darkest days of the German occupation in Paris" when he saw people lined up for hours to obtain scanty rations.

In Hopeh province peasants ate cottonseed cakes normally used as hog fodder. Although the Communists had eliminated prostitution in the early 1950s, girls in some places were reported to be selling themselves for food ration coupons. A nurse at a Peking hospital said the hospital canteen was serving "beef" that was really placenta from the maternity ward.

Hungry peasants stole from the fields and even raided state granaries. Some quit their communes to beg in the cities, to ambush trucks, or to rob travelers in the countryside. Beginning in 1959, when the food pinch first made itself felt, many neglected the grain crops of the collectives to raise vegetables and livestock that they could sell privately. These capitalist efforts were illegal; at first the selling was done covertly in the wee hours of morning. But soon peasants were coming into the city in broad daylight and there were too many peddlers and customers for the police to stop. Peasants got rich in the black market; in some communes half the collective land was being privately cultivated.

Official propaganda attributed China's food shortages and malnutrition to floods, droughts, and other natural calamities. But Liu Shao-ch'i, on a forty-four-day visit to Hunan province in the spring of 1961, explained privately that the problems were man-made.

By that time Liu and other Party leaders were working to remedy the situation left in the wake of Mao Tse-tung's Great Leap Forward. They launched a crash program to increase farm production, not with Maoist mobilization schemes, or Maoist orders to collect organic fertilizer, but with technical investment, and with a recognition, in Liu's words, that the prospect of capitalist tendencies appearing "is not so horrible."

Instead of bleeding the peasantry to finance heavy industry, as in the first Five-Year Plan, the Party bosses ordered factories to concentrate production on tractors, farm implements, irrigation equipment, and insecticides. Not only heavy-duty tractors, but simpler, flexible equipment suitable to specific topographical conditions and job requirements were ordered in a pragmatic effort to mechanize agriculture. Some 25,000 small workshops were established to produce threshers, huskers, harrows, tillers, multishare plows, and other tools that could be repaired simply in the field.

Modest sized fertilizer plants were built, and large amounts of chemical fertilizers were ordered from Belgium and Japan. The private farming and black market operations of The Great Leap Forward's hungry aftermath were legitimized, provided that the peasants fulfilled the grain and raw material output quotas recommended by the state.

If permitting some private enterprise involved a swallowing of Communist pride, so did the unprecedented step of buying grain from abroad. But beginning in the early 1960s, partly to feed China's coastal cities and thus relieve pressure on China's chaotic railway system, the Chinese began to buy 5 to 6 million tons of grain each year, principally wheat, and mainly from Australia and Canada.

This implicit confession of weakness in China's own grain production capability was especially significant in light of the growing schism between China and the Soviet Union. Said Mao, "the East wind is prevailing over the West wind." He meant that Soviet technological advances had swung the balance of power in favor of Communism, and he favored a tougher posture toward the United States, even if it provoked a nuclear war that might kill half of mankind. "The other half would remain," said Mao, "while imperialism would be razed to the ground, and the whole world would become socialist."

Khrushchev, who thought Mao's East wind so much hot air, openly denounced The Great Leap Forward in the late 1950s and in the summer of 1960 abruptly withdrew more than a thousand Russian technicians; he canceled the Soviet aid program.

But if China had pretensions of leadership in world Communism, Nikita Khrushchev, touring Hungary in the waning months of his power, made speeches in 1964 declaring that empty stomachs were not a good argument for Communism. He made sarcastic references to China's "empty rice bowls."

Had Nikita Sergeyevich stopped to think, he would

have realized that Chinese do not live by rice alone. The *Hun-t'un-pi* wrappings of wonton dumplings, especially popular in south China, are made of wheat flour. So are Chinese noodles (*mien*) and Mandarin *Po-ping* pancakes, to say nothing of egg rolls, spring rolls, steamed rolls, steamed buns, and steamed *dim sum* and *dien hsing* dumplings. Yes, and fortune cookies.

China, in fact, rivals India as the world's third largest wheat grower.

Within a year of Khrushchev's fall from power in Russia, Mao Tse-tung in China had renewed his efforts to mobilize the population, this time with his Great Proletarian Cultural Revolution. Denouncing the "revisionism" of Moscow, Mao used his Red Guards to impose a more purely Marxist brand of Communism on China.

Complicating Sino-Soviet relations now was the United States' presence in Vietnam, and a major factor in the Vietnamese struggle was rice, for which North Vietnam had until 1957 depended on South Vietnam. Hanoi's imitation of Peking's land reform program in the mid-1950s had been as ruinous to North Vietnam's agriculture as the original program had been to China's. Now China had to dig into its own rice pile to feed North Vietnam.

Mao had promised Premier Chou En-lai to exempt agriculture from his Cultural Revolution to avoid impeding production. But beginning early in 1967, Mao reneged on that promise.

For one thing, he set out to fulfill his dream of closing the old gap between China's intellectuals and her peasantry. In the *Hsia-fang* ("down to the countryside") movement, university graduates not otherwise needed were sent to rural areas, which most found dreary and monotonous. The peasants resented the eggheads. A commune in Kansu province rejected a contingent, saying they lacked farm experience, ate more than they could produce, and were a disruptive burden. A trainload of students arriving at a Kwangtung commune were promptly sent home. At another Kwangtung commune, four students were arrested and charged with "counterrevolutionary" sabotage when they accidentally broke some farm equipment they were using.

In some cases the young intellectuals were deprived of food rations and even beaten. Since country girls preferred urban workers, who lived better, the youths had trouble finding wives.

If the students had reason to despair during the Cultural Revolution, peasants had equal reason. Many were forced to work as temporary industrial workers at lower pay than regular workers and without their fringe benefits or family allowances. The higher-paid workers, in turn, were sent to the country and put to work at lower salaries. Although permanent factory workers received special rations, including meat and bean curd, peasants were not permitted to retain the food they cultivated.

Beginning with a Shanghai dock strike in December, 1966, the Cultural Revolution dissolved in 1967 into a virtual civil war. The strike spread to the northern parts of Dairen, Tientsin, and Tsingtao, which were unable to unload wheat, chemical fertilizers, and machinery, and unable to export rice, coal, and soybeans.

As in The Great Leap Forward, peasants in several provinces rebelled against the communes. They abandoned collective wheat and rice fields to cultivate private vegetable gardens; illegal black markets thrived with the produce of peasants selling at high prices. Communards refused to deliver grain to state purchasing agents and even plundered government grain stocks; in Kwangtung province, peasants reportedly intercepted a freight train and looted it for grain.

China-watchers in Hong Kong picked up a radio broadcast from Honan province; spring planting, said the radio, was "going very slowly" because rural cadres were "afraid to make mistakes and thus do not dare to lead boldly." Many "even lie down and do nothing. None of them cares about collective production."

In Szechwan, China's most populous (80 million) province and the nation's most fertile granary, urban dissidents recruited peasants to their cause, and the rustics looted shops and warehouses for goods not available in the country. By 1969 food production in the communes began to rise as they were reduced to more manageable size and their number increased from the original 26,000 of the Great Leap to about 78,000, with from 6,000 to 60,000 people in each. Some Leaplike moves were made after border clashes with Russia in March, 1969; if there was danger of a Sino-Soviet war, China needed a healthy, well-fed citizenry. Its communes were exhorted to develop small nitrogenous fertilizer plants, electric power stations, tool factories, iron foundries, steel furnaces, and other small decentralized enterprises that required relatively little investment. The war scare was used as an excuse to curb some private garden cultivation and "capitalist" marketing practices, and to obtain more wheat, rice, and other grain than procurement quotas required the communes to deliver.

But no rash overall programs were undertaken, and despite efforts by Party Vice-Chairman Lin Piao and other hawks to emphasize the production of sophisticated weaponry, Premier Chou En-lai and China's regional commanders invested China's meager resources in industry and agriculture.

By 1971, Chou was able to report that China's output of chemical fertilizer was rising and would be adequate for the nation's needs by 1975. Grain production, the best measure of success in agriculture, topped 240 million tons in 1970, up 25 percent from 1957, generally regarded as the previous peak year. Through rationing, rigorous procurement efforts, and those wheat imports from Australia, Canada, and other Western nations, China had managed to accumulate 40 million tons in grain reserves by the spring of 1971. And the 1971 crop totaled a record 250 million tons.

When Richard Nixon visited China in February, 1972, newsmen accompanying the President reported that food in the People's Republic was plentiful, cheap, and good. The American visitors saw live gray carp selling for 35 cents a pound in a Peking market. Stacks of freshly pressed duck were selling at about 4 yuan apiece, $1.70 at the going rate. (Peking factory workers received about 65 yuan a month—$27—but skilled workers got as much as 400 yuan—$170 a month.)

Dressed chicken fetched about 32 cents a pound and there was an abundance of live turkeys. Beef was about 30 cents a pound, causing some of the visitors to remember when beef in America had been cheaper than chicken. Mutton, pork, rabbit, and pheasants were also plentiful, and although there was no frozen produce, or in winter even refrigeration, there were plenty of fresh vegetables, including crisp radishes and spinach and stacks of white-colored cabbage priced at 5 cents a pound. Canned goods were on sale, including canned pineapple chunks. So was red wine, and a wine based on ginseng root.

According to the manager of the market, the food came "directly from the commune," whose brigade was composed of six production teams.

But it was still grain—mostly rice and wheat—that comprised the bulk of the Chinese diet, and rural peasantry that comprised 80 percent of the Chinese population.

In June, 1972, Peking reported that the northern provinces of Honan, Hopeh, and Shantung, more heavily populated (150 million combined) than any other Chinese provinces except Szechwan, were now basically self-sufficient in grain production. And in those northern provinces the grain was mostly wheat.

Harrison Salisbury of *The New York Times*, traveling in Honan at the time, said a drive in the northwest corner of the province was "like driving straight into the early 19th or late 18th century."

He reported seeing men and women in the fields, "bowed to the waist" and striding "swiftly through the high golden grain, cutting it with their scythes and quickly binding the sheaves with a strand of fiber, just as Americans did before the McCormick reaper."

He saw broad threshing floors of hard-baked clay with "hundreds of men, women, and children winnowing the wheat, tossing it into the air with wooden shovels and letting the wind separate the grain from the chaff, just as Americans did before the days of the threshing machine."

In what once had been arid and barren countryside, where "there was drought 9 years out of 10, and poor peasants traditionally sold their children and went out to beg to earn enough to escape starvation," Salisbury saw enormous irrigation projects, a fruitful country, and a healthy population.

Within a few months, however, Peking's optimism of

June had faded. There were reports of serious drought. By late fall, Chou was freely admitting to Western newsmen that the 1972 harvest of wheat, rice, and other cereals had fallen 10 million tons, a 4 percent decline from the 1971 harvest. Rumors circulated that the Chinese shortfall had actually been much greater, that the harvest was 10 percent below that of the previous year, a loss of 25 million tons.

In his fine book *Mao and China*, from which much of the information in this chapter derives, Stanley Karnow tells of a young Red Guard sent from south China to Peking during the Cultural Revolution. Given a string bag containing some slices of steamed bread, a few pieces of fruit, and three hard-boiled eggs to sustain him the following day, the youth eats his eggs right away but saves the unfamiliar steamed bread. Later, when he is hungry again, he finds the bread has hardened into inedible lumps.

Despite the difficulty of rice-eating southern Chinese to adopt many wheat flour foods, Peking, like Tokyo, has found it increasingly advantageous to earn hard currency by exporting rice while it imports wheat. So even with all the wheat it grows, mainland China imported between 4 and 7 million tons of wheat each year from 1962 to 1970. According to the Stanford Research Institute, the Chinese imported only 3.2 million tons in 1971, an indication that domestic wheat production had increased.

But in 1972 that production was reduced. Official Chinese sources late in November minimized the country's grain needs. The People's Republic, it was announced, still had 40 million tons of cereal grains in reserve. Yes, China had bought 5 million tons of grain, mostly from Australia and Canada, but it had exported 3 million tons of rice to countries such as Sri Lanka (Ceylon) and North

Vietnam. (Chinese rice is more widely acceptable than Japanese rice, which has only a small export market.)

Chou's pessimistic autumn revelations sparked a further rise in the price of U.S. wheat, already selling at a formidable $100 a ton. But China seemed bent more on saving face than on buying wheat.

As Morton Sosland's mysterious Mr. Smith had said back on August 10, the Chinese were negotiating with Louis Dreyfus; the French firm had representatives in Peking, but the Chinese were not buying. They were hoping prices would soften.

But even with her campaign to lower birth rates, China's population was growing. We must "wash away the influence of erroneous ideas, such as that many children means lots of happiness," said the Szechwan provincial Revolutionary Committee; but each month there were $2\frac{1}{2}$ million more Chinese mouths to feed.

A two-month shipping strike had delayed imports from Canada, and in late September, too late for a wheat exporter to receive subsidy on U.S. wheat, China finally came to terms: Peking bought 400,000 tons of U.S. soft red winter and West Coast white wheat through Dreyfus.

It was the first Chinese-American grain transaction in more than twenty years. And it was soon followed by a 300,000 ton sale.

Late in November, Dreyfus agents in Peking were told that foreign dealers were inflating wheat prices artificially because they knew China was in the market.

"They want us to pay more, but they will be disappointed," said an official of the state Foodstuffs Import-Export Corporation.

China would wait until prices came down, even if it meant tightening her belt.

Prices—and futures—did move lower and in March,

1973, Peking bought another 400,000 tons of wheat, plus an equal amount of corn, for delivery between July and September. The purchase was made through the French firm of Louis Dreyfus, which, in a face-saving maneuver, was given the option of supplying grain from the United States.

Rice rations in Canton had been reduced 6.6 percent on January 1, and radio broadcasts had reportedly stressed the importance of saving grain "in preparation for war and natural disasters." Party Chairman Mao, in a New Year's directive, had called on the people to "dig tunnels deep" and to "store grain everywhere."

13.

Ten bushels of wheat grow in the world for every bushel of rye. What rye is grown chiefly comes from Russia, which raises nearly half the world's crop. Rye will ripen where the season is too short for wheat; and in much of Russia the season is far too short.

But while dark Russian peasant bread is thus often rye bread, or pumpernickel, most of the basic Russian breads—and no other country has such a repertoire of bread variations—are made from wheat flour dough.

Agnautka, that flat whole-grained loaf, is a wheat bread. The two-foot round white mound called *polianitsa,* with its crusty cap, is a wheat bread. So is *Ukrainka,* the heavy dark cartwheel-shaped bread, rough-textured and weighing three pounds to a loaf.

And Russians eat wheat not only in breads but in pancakes, dumplings, pastries, cakes, buns, even in *kasha,* which is often made from the groats (broken up hulled grains) of wheat and other grains as well as of buckwheat.

Pancakes may be the familiar *bliny,* or the dessert

pancakes called *pannkogid*. Dumplings run the gamut from *palmeni*, stuffed with mashed potatoes, meat, cheese, or vegetables, to *vareniki*, the traditional dessert dumplings. *Pirozhki* and *kulebiaka* are pastries as beloved by commissars as they once were by czars and czarinas.

Bulochky, palochky, pampushky, balabushky—the names of the crumb sprinkled buns, the soft seed bread sticks, the doughnut puffs, the sourdough rolls tumble off the tongue like a Danny Kaye lyric.

Of Russian rolls and buns there is no end: the sweet buns (*zdoba*), the twisted buns (*kruchenyk*), the bagel-like hard rolls (*bublyky*), the almond horns (*rohalyky*), the little horns (*rizhok.*)

It is bread, plain and fancy, that serves as the staff of Russian life, from basic mother's bread (*deda's puri*) and triple braided twist bread (*khala*), to unsweetened white bread (*khorz*), bread sticks (*solomka*), and the Easter treat of *koulitch*.

The names are strange to American ears. And they are but the beginning. About 200 different kinds of bread are made in the Soviet Union; the Moscow Central Bakeries alone turn out 130 varieties. The average Russian eats a pound of *khleb* a day; in some rural areas he eats even more, although consumption has declined slightly in recent years. The average American, by comparison, eats far less bread than he did years ago. Flour consumption in the United States averages 110 pounds a year per capita, of which 90 pounds goes into baked goods such as bread; using three-quarters of a pound of flour to make a pound loaf of bread, 90 pounds of flour translates into 120 pounds of bread a year, less than a third the Russian consumption.

The wheat that made the flour that went into many of Russia's breads, rolls, buns, cakes, pastries, dumplings, and pancakes in 1973 was hard red winter wheat from Kansas, Nebraska, Texas, and Oklahoma.

According to John Smith, the Russians were terribly concerned lest their grain-buying be construed as evidence that the Communist system was not working. This, he said, had much to do with their desire for secrecy.

But the malfunctioning of the system in the U.S.S.R. has been observed by Soviet leaders as well as by outsiders. The British Soviet expert, Max Hayward, has said, "The Red Army is the only efficient organization in the whole Soviet Union." The least efficient segment of the economy has been the Soviet food production apparatus.

In July, 1970, the Central Committee of the Communist party approved a report condemning mismanagement in Soviet agriculture. The report was submitted by none other than Party Chief Leonid I. Brezhnev. It admitted that Soviet supplies of food were inadequate and promised increased production of grains, meat, vegetables, and other foods.

Food production, said Brezhnev, had increased since 1965, when he and Premier Aleksei N. Kosygin had taken over control of the Party and government from Nikita S. Khrushchev; it would increase further in the five-year period beginning in January, 1971. By 1975, said Brezhnev, the average annual production of grains would increase to 195 million tons, as compared with a yearly average of 162 million tons in the previous five years. Meat production would go from 11.4 million tons to 15.6 million.

"The situation in grain production still does not satisfy us," declared Brezhnev. "The amount of vegetables and fruits grown is inadequate. As we all know, the demand of the population for livestock produce, especially meat, is not being satisfied by far."

He promised an increase of 70 percent, about $85 billion, in capital investment, and improved state and party control of agriculture.

"The expansion of the material and technical basis of the collective and state farms is one of our most important tasks," said the Brezhnev report. "The carrying out of this task is most closely linked with the need for improving the everyday practical guidance of agriculture by government and party bodies, and with a more vigorous struggle against the lack of responsibility and discipline, and mismanagement."

To what extent was it weather, and to what extent irresponsibility and mismanagement, that caused the 1972 crop shortfalls in the Soviet Union?

For 1972, the Soviet grain production goal was set at 190 million tons; on December 21, speaking at a meeting to commemorate the fiftieth anniversary of the U.S.S.R., party leader Brezhnev gave the official figure for the grain harvest: 168 million tons.

This was 22 million short of the announced goal, but it was well above the 162 million ton average of the late 1960s. Some Western experts estimated that Brezhnev's figure was too high, that the Soviet harvest had really been only 160 million tons. Nobody knows, possibly not even the Russians.

In his December 21 speech, Brezhnev announced that the state had purchased 30 million tons of grain from abroad. Food supplies would be maintained he said, "the normal course of the life of the country and its citizens will not be disrupted."

There was evidence in Soviet newspapers that the

"normal course of life" in Russia left something to be desired. As early as late August, 1972, while capitalist speculators were bidding up commodity futures prices on the Chicago and Kansas City markets, Muscovites were complaining that good potatoes had become almost impossible to find.

"If it's this bad now," said a man waiting in one of the capital's long queues, "you can expect it will be worse in winter."

In early September the Communist party daily *Pravda* disclosed stoppages in bread supplies to a number of towns in the Gorky region, 250 miles east of Moscow. Some collective and state farms in the north Caucasus around Stavropol were accused of having stopped all grain deliveries to the state for twenty-five days in August. Said *Pravda*, "the interests of the state are put in the background and preference is given to local interests."

Another paper criticized farms for permitting a sharp drop-off in milk production. It charged that some cows were producing 200 pounds less milk than in normal years, and that some farms were 150 to 300 tons below their planned production levels.

What no paper mentioned was that the Soviet Union, usually a seller in the world grain market, had invaded its gold reserves to buy from the West.

Big grain and potato purchases were negotiated with other Eastern bloc countries. But Soviet crop shortfalls were greater than could be made up by East Germany, Bulgaria, Hungary, Poland, or Romania. Even with a tightening of belts in the Baltic states and in Byelorussia, there would not be enough to satisfy the demands of Moscow.

Still, there were official statements that no real emergency existed. *Moskva,* the Moscow evening newspaper, said Soviet citizens would "never hear the words 'no bread' that our people used to hear during the war."

There were, at the same time, exhortations not to waste bread. And there were reports of hoarding.

Appearing on Moscow television, Deputy Mayor Leonid V. Deribin said, "There are some Muscovites who, despite the obvious facts, still believe the capital will run short of potatoes and now seek to stash away their own supply." Such panic buying, he said, was "totally unjustified." Government storage facilities were far superior to those in Moscow homes, and those who made bulk purchases were risking spoilage losses.

As far south as Kharkov in the Ukraine, consumers were bracing for a lean winter. Moscow ordered rapid expansion of refrigerated warehouses; it set up special motor pools to ferry shipments coming in to storage depots from other parts of the Soviet Union. Railroad workers were told they had "special obligations" to handle vast cargoes of potatoes, cabbage, and other food staples before the October frosts set in.

But in late September, with the wheat harvest still only one-third completed in a few key areas, the season's first snow was reported from northern Kazakhstan. No Western newsmen were permitted to visit Kazakhstan, nor were any allowed in Siberia, or in the Urals, but Russian press reports depicted a chaotic situation in those regions.

Pravda ran a headline that said, "Time is pressing the grain farmer." A dispatch from Tselinograd, in the heart of the Kazakhstan wheat country, sounded an ominous note: "We are in the last ten days of September—that says everything. And the first snow should be a stern warning."

Who could blame any Russian for recalling the old days of wartime food shortages? Some elderly people remembered the terrible famine of 1921, when 3 million in the Volga valley died of starvation and many more were saved only by the private relief efforts organized by Herbert Hoover.

The Soviet economy had collapsed in 1921; to placate the peasants Lenin adopted a New Economic Policy (NEP) that abolished the food levy, introduced a limited grain tax, and—in 1922—for the first time permitted small private farms to supplement the collective and state farm system. During the summer of 1972 private farmers were flying into Moscow (air fares are cheap in the Soviet Union) with their suitcases full of produce from Georgia and Tashkent. Even in a good year there would be little in the way of fruit and vegetables come winter, but a shortage of potatoes, of bread? Reports of those scarcities chilled the heart.

Wrestling with inflation in the United States, President Nixon had inaugurated a New Economic Policy of his own just the year before; but the price controls he imposed did not cover unprocessed commodity foods such as potatoes and wheat.

In September, 1972, prices of those commodities were hitting record highs in America. In the case of potatoes, poor crops were the main factor. Not so with wheat. The wheat harvest, more than one-fourth of it already sold to Russia, was close to its all-time high. It was coming in at 1.54 billion bushels (about 42 million metric tons), only 73 million bushels below the record 1971 crop, 32 million below the previous high of 1968.

In the Soviet Union the picture was quite different, even in Kazakhstan. Khrushchev had been warned that rainfall was undependable in that province, and in some years it had been; but in 1972 the problem was too much rain. Wet wheat, said *Pravda*, was being gathered in

Kazakhstan under drizzly skies; grain elevators, lacking equipment to dry the wheat, were refusing it. And although thousands of trucks had been commandeered from the cities there were still not enough to move the wheat to storage bins.

But in mid-October the Soviet press reported that Kazakhstan had produced a record crop of 27 million tons, 1.5 million tons over the previous record set in 1966. About 60 percent of the grain had reportedly been delivered to the state grain marketing agency for distribution to city millers and to areas short of grain; the remaining 40 percent would be retained in Kazakhstan for seed grain, livestock feed, and local consumption. Western experts noted that wet grain weighs more than dry, that the 27 million ton figure was no doubt watered a certain amount, but even taking this into account it looked like the Kazakhstan harvest had made up for much of the Ukraine shortfall.

Weather conditions were largely to blame for the poor crops of the Ukraine but there were reports, too, of mismanagement. These were given credence February 1 when *Pravda* announced that the chief of the Russian Republic's conglomerate for selling farm equipment and supplies had been fired. He was charged with "violating state discipline," and the wording of the *Pravda* report suggested that he might face trial.

Two days later Vladimir Matskevich got the ax. Tass, the Soviet press agency, reported that the agriculture minister who had played host to Earl Butz and Clarence Palmby the previous spring had been "relieved" of his post by the Supreme Soviet. His replacement was Dmitri S. Polyansky, Matskevich's superior in the powerful Politburo, who was demoted from his position as first deputy premier and given direct control of the Agriculture Ministry.

Production not only of grain but of milk, sugar, and cooking oils had fallen below 1971 levels. As of January 1, Soviet hog holdings had been cut back from 71.4 million to 66.5 million for lack of feed. So while some other livestock herds had increased, and egg production was up, there was evidence of a farm crisis, which the Kremlin was tacitly acknowledging.

As *New York Times* correspondent Hedrick Smith reported, "Such high-level demotions have been extremely unusual in recent years and underscore both the regime's acute embarrassment over the agricultural failures and the serious problems that these failures have created for the economy as a whole, including the lowering of general economic targets for 1973."

If Soviet agriculture was being inefficiently managed, as the demotions suggested, other parts of the Soviet economy were no less so. At the end of October, when ships full of foreign grain were arriving at Baltic and Black Sea ports, Soviet railways were swamped with grain from the country's domestic harvest. Moreover, the Soviet newspaper on maritime affairs, *Vodny Transport*, said grain imports at Riga were being held up by lack of cooperation between railway men and port authorities. The Soviet railways were supplying only 41 percent of the boxcars ordered; traffic controllers were dispatching empty cars according to a fixed timetable and not in response to need; it was taking longer to process the boxcars' documents than to load up the cars; the cars were often not equipped with proper covers and were being sent on their way with grain leaking out their self-sealing doors.

"Cargo Number One," as the Russians called the Western grain, was having a hard time.

In late January, 1973, Moscow published figures showing that Russia's Gross National Product had grown by only 4 percent in 1972; this was the lowest growth rate in a decade and well short of the 6.2 percent target.

Personal income in the Soviet Union had increased by 3.7 percent against a goal of 5.2 percent; even after the increase, according to the government newspaper *Izvestia*, the average Soviet worker in an office or factory (whose output was less than half that of his opposite number in America) earned only 130.33 rubles ($157.66) per month.

Opportunities for spending those earnings were still limited. For although Leonid Brezhnev had spoken two years earlier of "saturating the market with consumer goods," *Izvestia* criticized Soviet industry for producing poor quality merchandise in narrow variety; shoes, clothing, and home appliances, the very items Brezhnev had promised would lead the U.S.S.R. into the consumer era, were those in shortest supply. For despite the official rhetoric about consumer goods, the real emphasis in Soviet production was on energy production, heavy power, steel, machine building, transport, and engineering. In these basic industries the 1972 growth rate targets had been met whereas the consumer goods sector, including food, had lagged behind. Khruschev's "metal eaters" were still calling the shots (at least 40 percent of the nation's economy, according to unofficial Soviet sources, is producing directly or indirectly for the military).

Meat supplies became more plentiful in Moscow in late 1972 and early 1973, an indication that peasants were killing off livestock for lack of feed. Russians, as usual, ate less meat than Western Europeans, and some basic commodities such as butter and potatoes were reportedly rationed in parts of the country, but not bread.

Soviet grain production for 1972 may have been 16 million tons short of the 1971 crop, but if we accept Brezhnev's figure it totaled above the average for the five years from 1966 to 1970. Even if the figure is adjusted to allow for poor quality and high moisture content at harvest time, the U.S.S.R. had reaped tremendous tonnages of wheat, rye, oats, barley, corn, and grain sorghums.

Were the 30 million tons purchased in the world market really necessary for Russia's internal needs? Is it possible that Comrades Belousov, Kalitenko, and Sakun were buying more than they needed to keep Peking from getting that Western grain?

14.

One thing was certain. However efficient U.S. agriculture may be, and whatever that efficiency may owe to a competitive free-enterprise economy, it was the free market system that enabled the Russian purchasing agents to buy so much U.S. grain without having Americans find out about it.

Had the deals been made with Argentina, Australia, or Canada, the Russians would have had to negotiate with government monopolies; they would have been unable to fragment purchases among six private firms, with none of the six knowing what the others had sold, and with the U.S. Department of Agriculture too long in the dark about the entire matter.

When some criticism of the Soviet wheat deal was leveled at the Nixon administration in the fall of 1972, Senate Republican leader Hugh Scott said the attack was spurred by people associated with the Canadian Wheat Board.

"They want the United States to come to a Canadian Wheat Board type of operation," he said. "Under the Canadian system, the farmer wouldn't get a thing."

Scott's viewpoint was shared by Ohio's Republican senator, William Saxbe, who said that the export sales under the Canadian system would come from government surplus stocks, and the only benefit would be to the government.

The Canadian Wheat Board is a populist-socialist development that grew out of the great agricultural depression of the 1920s. Farmers in that era set up cooperatives they called "pools." And out of the Manitoba Pool, the Alberta Pool, the Saskatchewan Pool, the British Columbia Pool, came the Wheat Board, a centralized agency that guarantees farmers a minimum price for their wheat and, at the end of the year, divides up profits in shares proportionate to the amount of wheat each farmer delivered to the board that year.

Senators Scott and Saxbe were dead set against any such Wheat Board in the United States. Agriculture Secretary Butz agreed.

"If the government provided the service which the grain trade renders," he said, "it would certainly be at a cost. In fact, I shudder to think of the cost if the government provided the service . . .

"We will continue to depend upon the private sector of the American economy to conduct the export marketing of our farm products. The grain trade is one of the most fiercely competitive industries in this country. That competition benefits the farmer and the public."

He did not mention that on July 24, 1972, both the Australian and Canadian Wheat Boards, evidently well aware of how much wheat Moscow had bought from America, had urged the USDA to stop export subsidies and permit the world price of wheat to reach its realistic level.

Butz's friendly attitude toward the big private grain

exporters was dramatized within a few weeks when a question arose about giving those export firms a tax break on their profits.

Under a 1971 law, designed to keep industry from leaving the United States, a corporation with overseas earnings could defer taxes indefinitely on half those earnings provided it reinvested them in overseas trade. The law gave the Treasury Department discretionary authority to deny this tax break to a company whose exports had already been subsidized by the United States.

Since the exporters had been granted $300 million in subsidies on the wheat they sold to foreign nations, including the U.S.S.R., the Treasury on October 4, 1972, issued tentative regulations denying them the special tax relief.

Continental, Cargill, and the other export companies protested. They said the law, in its reference to exports already subsidized, was talking about concessional sales such as those made through the Agency for International Development; it was not referring to sales made on ordinary commercial terms.

Cargill argued that foreign trade was subsidized in a variety of ways, that to merchandise U.S. wheat successfully an export company needed both export subsidies and tax benefits. Supporting this position were the chairmen of the Senate Finance and Agriculture committees.

Another supporter was the USDA's assistant secretary for international affairs, Carroll Brunthaver.

Grain traders, said Brunthaver, needed the tax break "to more effectively compete with suppliers from other countries which offer commodities for export at reduced prices.

"Even if you do not concur in the legal position of the Agriculture Department," he said, Treasury should not use its discretionary power to deny the tax relief to grain traders.

When Treasury prevailed, it was charged with knuckling under to political pressures. To keep export companies from moving abroad, said their supporters, would require help from U.S. taxpayers. That was one of the prices of the free enterprise system.

Defenders of the system said it would be disastrous to put U.S. grain exports under the control of a government agency. To illustrate what they meant by "disastrous," they pointed to U.S. Army procurement and to the U.S. Postal Service.

But it could be argued, and it was, that the "free" U.S. economy was already something of a planned economy, that some government control was necessary, and that the secrecy surrounding Exportkhleb's grain buying had worked to the disadvantage of taxpayers, to say nothing of farmers and the food-buying public. The competitive capitalist system, whatever its undeniable blessings, had permitted the concealment that played into Moscow's hands. In 1973 even Wall Street, traditionally opposed to government controls, was crying for more controls.

The Communists were credited with a superb understanding of the free market economy, which they exploited to their advantage. The Russians' insistence on such tight security, said their admirers, was part of their strategem. But to some extent the surreptitious nature of their buying may have been dictated simply by an apprehension of criticism of Soviet agriculture.

It was the weather, said the Russians, the worst in a hundred years, and not any defect in the collective farm system that produced 1972's need for such enormous grain imports. But quite aside from considerations of weather, of a creaky farm system, of general Soviet inefficiency, and of a vestigial capitalistic delight in putting over a big deal, there is a nagging suspicion that John Smith may have been right in his theory that grain was being used as a diplomatic ploy in the struggle between the two giants of the Communist world.

Six months after Nikolai Belousov's Exportkhleb bought 20 million tons of U.S. grain, three-quarters of that grain was still sitting in U.S. farmers' bins, in U.S. grain elevators, and in U.S. railroad cars. Delayed earlier by haggling over shipping terms, deliveries were now bogged down in rail-transit troubles.

While many rail-cars sat idle in the East, a shortage of cars in the West was causing what the traffic manager of a country elevator group called "the worst mess I've seen in the twenty years I've been in this business. We're grabbing anything we can get our hands on—coal cars, baggage cars, anything that will hold a bushel of grain."

Open-hopper cars, normally used to haul coal, were authorized for grain hauling by the Interstate Commerce Commission, which said railroads could charge the same rates they charged for the larger covered-hopper cars ordinarily employed in grain transport. Another 20,000 open-hoppers were available, although they would have to be cleaned and in many cases repaired so that grain would not trickle out their bottoms. Unless they were tightly covered with tarpaulins, the open-hoppers would permit damage to the grain from rain and snow; but in the rush to deliver grain, some cars went off to the ports with their grain exposed.

At the Gulf ports, huge machines picked up boxcars and shook them back and forth to make their wheat pour out onto conveyor belts that carried it into grain elevators. Unloading a boxcar took eight minutes, much longer than to unload a hopper car. To unload the 900 boxcars that were needed to fill one big ship took almost five days.

Longshoremen at the Gulf ports, while not boycotting Russian ships as they had done in 1964 because they were "Red," were not responding to shapeup calls because they despised the work of "trimming" grain in Russian tanker holds, a hot dirty job essential to avoid unbalanced loads that could make ships keel over. The men preferred the big bargelike bulk carriers on which grain is distributed evenly by gravity through long steel spouts and a man has little to do but watch. Because of loading delays, ships waited up to forty-five days before they could steam up the fifty-mile-long Houston ship channel and berth at loading docks.

The ports of Houston, New Orleans, Pascagoula, Mississippi, and Mobile were clogged with thousands of railcars waiting to unload. On the Illinois Central Gulf Railroad, cars that had taken ten days to make the round trip from country elevator to port and back were taking fifteen to twenty days.

The delays were costing shippers upwards of 2 cents a bushel in demurrage—charges for detention of ships and rail-cars beyond specified periods of time. Export companies were faced with losses: export subsidies on winter wheat would expire May 31. But an official of a grain-hauling railroad predicted it would be "at least until the end of 1973 before we get all this grain moved."

Nebraska's Republican senator, Carl Curtis, called it "the most serious breakdown in transportation in the history of the United States."

Anxious about deliveries, Nikolai Belousov returned to America in late January and spent two weeks visiting Gulf ports in an effort to get more grain moving. He was finally persuaded in New York to accept ergot-free spring wheat, on which export subsidies would not expire until August, in place of some winter wheat.

"We should have been hauling this wheat last August," said a Port of Houston grain elevator manager, "but they were arguing about which countries' ships were going to transport it."

The real victims of the jam that tied up the rail-cars were U.S. farmers and consumers.

Where local elevators were obliged to ship by truck instead of by rail, they were often unable to pay farmers the grain prices quoted at Chicago, Minneapolis, or Kansas City. The situation did not encourage these farmers to increase their planted acreage. Some farmers did not receive shipments of feed grain they had ordered. Many faced delays in fertilizer shipments. Anhydrous ammonia, diammonia phosphate, urea, and other nitrogen fertilizers are usually shipped in covered-hopper cars, the same kind preferred for shipping grain. U.S. farmers use more than $2.5 billion worth of these fertilizers a year, and most of it moves during a six-week period in midspring. But in midspring of 1973 the competition for closed-hopper cars was fierce. Grain exporters, more than four months behind schedule on their shipments to Russia, were clamoring for more cars before their export subsidies expired. Fertilizer companies, which needed new or well-maintained closed-hopper cars to prevent leakage, were told they could expect only half the number they usually got. And 1973 was not a usual year.

Despite higher prices, the demand for fertilizer was the highest in recent memory. Farmers wanted to boost their yields to take advantage of higher commodity prices, and that would take fertilizer. Spring planting would have to be completed by May 30, and fertilizer would have to be applied well before that date. But in a nation whose rail-cars were occupied with Russian grain shipments, the logistics of shipping fertilizer were dimming the outlook for higher yields that could help hold down 1974 food prices.

Railroad tie-ups were also boosting transportation costs of food and other freight. And by blocking grain shipments, the rail jam was putting incredible pressure on grain elevators and flour millers, who had to borrow vast amounts of money from banks to finance their operations while they waited to collect on grain they had sold or to maintain margins on wheat futures they had sold. Interest charges on these loans were increasing their cost of operations; that cost would inevitably be passed on to consumers and be reflected in higher food prices.

15.

When Mary Jones went to her supermarket one day in November, 1972, she found eggs selling for 61 cents a dozen. Hadn't they been only 50 cents in the spring?

The Jones family uses a dozen and a half eggs a week, the national average (it bought more before Mr. Jones got worried about cholesterol and cut down).

The following week eggs cost 66 cents a dozen and the week after that 71 cents. Mrs. Jones hoped the rise was just temporary but at Christmas eggs were 76 cents a dozen and the week after that 81 cents.

America has about 440 million chickens, two for every person, and nearly three out of four are raised solely to lay eggs. Egg prices almost always go up in the winter as hens, clinging to inherited cyclical traits, defy modern poultry management techniques and lay fewer eggs. But in the winter of 1972–73, as Mrs. Jones found, U.S. egg prices were climbing at an extraordinary rate.

There were a number of reasons for this rise, but the chief one was simply that farmers had reduced their laying flocks. In 1969 and early 1970 when egg prices climbed as high as $1 a dozen, farmers had ordered new laying hens at a tremendous rate. But Americans were eating no more eggs than usual; the national average remained at 300 per year per capita. And a new vaccine, introduced early in 1971, was eliminating Marek's disease, a malignancy with a high fatality rate that had been wiping out 15 to 20 percent of the hens each year. Some 50 million hens, each laying about 240 eggs a year, were saved by the vaccine.

With so many more hens laying, the glut of eggs forced prices down below the cost of production. But egg farmers reacted by engaging in a deliberate, desperate, and for many a suicidal effort to force out competition, much as the A&P would do with its WEO program two years later. After two years of chicken-farm bankruptcies, the Senate Agriculture Committee approved an egg industry adjustment bill that would require each producer to slaughter a percentage of his hens after any three-month period in which eggs sold below production costs.

Paul Findley, the Illinois congressman who later introduced a bill to end the tax on bread, decried the egg bill in a House speech that sounded as if Art Buchwald had written it.

"Imagine the cluckings Ralph Nader and his raiders will give forth when they hear of henocide," Findley orated.

"But loud as may be these cluckings, they will be smothered to nothing in feather-flying fury when gals of Women's Lib discover this ugly ultimate in male chauvinism. They will surely ungirdle their sharpest clawings for those who do nothing—not even harmless, painless vasectomy—to the males, the perpetrators of overproduction. Surely they will bare their beaks and demand roostercide instead of henocide.

"Plucked down to bare facts, this bill is nothing more

than a scheme to use the lethal authority of Government to force up the market price of eggs by killing hens. It will set up an eggopoly able to get the feds to man the chopping block with penalties to violators set at $5,000 a cackle. With antitrust immunity, the eggopoly could engage in a premeditated conspiracy to raise consumer prices with hardly any fuss and feathers."

But the bill passed, and the egg industry emerged from its two-year depression. Even had the bill not passed, laying flocks would have been cut. For one thing, a poultry virus infection called exotic Newcastle disease had come into the country (especially into southern California) from Britain and Europe and had necessitated the slaughter of 9 million hens, 3 percent of the U.S. flock, in just twelve weeks.

America still had 100,000 egg farms but just 10,000 of them produced 75 to 80 percent of the nation's eggs. Those farms that remained untouched by Newcastle disease were reducing flocks simply by not replacing hens as they became too old to lay. Normally such hens were sold for stewing and to chicken-pot-pie freezers, but egg farmers pinched by the two-year production wars had little money left to buy new hens. Many recycled older birds (seventeen to twenty-one months is old) with a force-molting process. Hens molt naturally in the fall, when they lose their feathers and halt their egg production for a month or so. A farmer can induce molt by giving hens the hormone progesterone, by feeding or injecting thyroid materials, or by removing a bird's water supply for a day and her feed for three or four days. A hen that has laid eggs for twelve to fifteen months, if force-molted, will stop laying for six to eight weeks but will then resume laying for nine or ten months more, although less efficiently than before because she will require more expensive feed.

Feed prices were sky-high in late 1972 and much of

1973, partly because grain sales to Russia had tightened the supply situation. Even if there had been no end to the ruinous production war, even if there had been no Newcastle disease, egg prices had to reflect the higher cost of corn and soybean meal. Some of the extra nickels that Mrs. Jones and shoppers all across the country were paying for eggs went to defray the higher cost of chicken feed.

A North Branch, New York, farmer, whose 250,000-bird flock made him about the 110th largest U.S. egg producer, complained to an interviewer that feed prices had "risen drastically since the sale of feed to Russia and China." He claimed that "speculators took advantage of the crops being sold to the Russians and Chinese" to drive up feed prices.

But while egg futures rigging has been connected with higher supermarket egg prices, nobody has proved that feed grain futures were manipulated or that such manipulation, if any, could have pushed up chicken feed prices. These prices are largely determined by fundamental factors of supply and demand. By shortening supplies of corn and soybeans, the Russian buying in the summer of 1972 helped to raise feed prices. Many other factors were undoubtedly involved in the rising price of eggs, but one factor was certainly higher feed prices.

Eggs, which may or may not have come first, lead to chickens—boiled, broiled, fricasseed, fried, roasted, and stewed. Chicken was once so expensive that it was reserved for Sunday dinner, recalling the seventeenth-century French king's wish that every peasant be able to afford "a chicken in his pot every Sunday." But in recent years the efficiency of U.S. poultry-raising while making chicken virtually tasteless, has also made chicken cheaper than any red meat.

With 6 percent of the world's population, America raises about a fifth of the world's chickens and turkeys; Americans eat six times more chicken than before World War II.

President Richard Nixon, early in 1973, polished off a dish of red snapper in Florida and urged his countrymen to eat fish rather than beef. Eating fish, he said, was "patriotic." Had he looked at fish prices he would have seen that they were higher even than beef, partly because Russian and East European trawlers and factory ships were taking fish in such quantity from U.S. coastal waters. Red herrings were in plentiful supply, but edible fish had grown scarcer and costlier.

Chicken was much cheaper than fish or red meat. Housewives were cooking chicken with avocados, bananas, almond slivers, pitted cherries, prunes, grapes, sour cream, white wine, herbs such as rosemary, and fancy sauces to give it taste and variety. Chicken was enabling them to make ends meet.

But from as little as 24 cents a pound in some supermarkets in June, 1972, the price of broilers (which are more often fried than broiled) had doubled by early 1973. Wholesale poultry prices were at near record levels throughout the country.

Chicken was still about half the price of hamburger, as it had been for years, but that was simply because hamburger had become so costly. In Springdale, Arkansas, a major producer predicted that poultry prices would increase another 6 to 7 cents per pound in 1973, and he singled out higher feed prices as the reason.

Along with bad harvest weather in the Corn Belt and the disappearance of anchovies off the coast of Peru, Don Tyson of Tyson foods mentioned "the Russian grain deal" as a major cause of higher feed prices. Chicken production, he said, would drop 3 to 5 percent because feed was so expensive.

If feed prices are a big factor in the cost of raising beef and hogs, they are also a big factor in a poultryman's costs. It takes from 6 to 8 pounds of grain to produce one pound of steer (live weight), and 4 to 5 pounds to produce one pound of live hog. Poultry raising is more efficient. In 1941, when every farmer's wife kept a flock of chickens, it took 4½ pounds of feed to produce a pound of live chicken (which came to .72 pounds ready to cook). By 1950, as the use of newly-developed health products permitted concentrated poultry farming with much less risk of flock-decimating disease, the ratio dropped to about 3 to 1; by 1969 it was down to 1.8 pound of ration to a pound of live weight and going lower. But to produce a pound of ready-to-cook chicken still took nearly 2½ pounds of feed.

Raising 30,000 birds at a time, selling them at eight to ten weeks of age (before they had time to develop much flavor, unfortunately), a single poultryman could raise from 150,000 to 195,000 broilers a year. Wages were hardly a factor. Not much land was required. The economics of converting chicken feed into broilers depended mainly on the price of corn and soybeans.

According to the National Broiler Council, "43 percent of chicken costs are bound up in feeds—65 percent in corn, 25 percent in soybean meal." When wholesale broiler prices jumped from 14½ cents a pound live weight to 23⅓ cents live weight, it was partly because rising red meat costs had shifted demand to poultry. But it was mostly because corn had gone from less than 2 cents a pound to nearly 2½ cents, and because soybeans had soared from 53 cents a pound to more than a dollar.

Poultrymen cut back flocks 5 percent in December, 1972, and cut them back again in the early months of 1973. Some producers increased their flocks as live poultry prices rose, but since it takes about three months to increase the supply of broilers it would be fall at the earliest before the picture could be turned around.

"There is a hesitancy to increase production because of the feed price situation," said the National Broiler Council's director of economic research. "The question is not whether [feed] prices will rise but how much higher they are going to rise. We are just reflecting production levels where you can stay in business. As long as ingredient prices remain high and until we can recover from [flock] reductions, we will continue to have high chicken prices."

Housewives could save by buying whole birds instead of breasts or legs, or by buying specials on five-pound boxes of legs or breasts, by buying bigger turkeys (which have more meat in proportion to bone than chickens), by knowing that the oil, water, flavors, fats, and phosphates injected into self-basting turkeys cost as much per pound as the turkey itself.

But all the shopping and cooking expertise in the world could not get around the fact that poultry prices reflected feed prices, and that feed prices reflected the grain and soybean purchases some Russians at the New York Hilton had made in the summer of 1972.

16.

"Give a man a fish and you feed him for a day. Show him how to fish and you feed him the rest of his days."

The Chinese proverb meant more when the world's seas, lakes, and rivers were still clean and unexploited; when the planet was still thinly peopled; when life was harder but simpler.

As W. S. Gilbert said in *Patience,* "There's fish in the sea, no doubt of it, as good as ever came out of it."

But on the shore there are now far more mouths to be fed. And although the Chinese proverb stresses self-sufficiency, national self-sufficiency in food production is not always desirable, at least not in peacetime. Not if it is achieved at the sacrifice of other consumer objectives.

Self-sufficiency too often means inefficiency. Efficient agriculture, by eliminating the need for so many farm workers, has created social upheaval, as we have seen, by driving untrained rural people into the cities. But the world can no longer afford inefficient agriculture. With populations growing, and the amount of arable land shrinking, with the eternal uncertainties of the weather, each acre, each hectare of land must be made to yield as many bushels, as many quintals of food as is possible within the limits of good soil management, environmental well-being, and economic realities.

Countries such as Belgium and the Netherlands, using intensive agriculture, achieve enormous grain yields per unit of land. Japan, if it chose to, could probably feed its people without importing grain, but it would require an intense input of capital and labor that makes no economic sense, not when the capital and labor can be used more profitably, and when grain can be imported cheaply.

This reasoning is easy to advance when you live in America. No other country has such a contiguous land mass of fertile soil watered by adequate rainfall through a long growing season. No other country has so many well-capitalized farms, so much reserve acreage that is kept out of production, so much efficient farm machinery.

The U.S.S.R., by comparison, is a marginal agricultural power. It has vast areas of arable land, but the frost-free growing season is short even in the south. In Krasnodar in the north Caucasus, the season is 190 days, the same as in Omaha, Nebraska. Around Kharkov, in the Ukraine, it is 150 days, only slightly longer than in Duluth, Minnesota. Around Moscow it is 130 days, the equivalent of the northern part of North Dakota.

Soviet yields do not approach those achieved in America, partly because yields of spring wheat, Russia's major crop, are only about half those of winter wheat. In 1971, the U.S.S.R. had a good crop year; wheat production was 82 million tons. But the wheat yield was only 12.8 quintals per hectare. (A hectare is 2.471 acres, a quintal is a hundredweight—100 kilograms, or roughly 220 pounds.) The United States in 1971 raised a record 44 million tons of wheat; the average yield was 21.7 quintals per hectare.

In 1972 the Soviet yield was only an estimated 10.4 quintals, versus 20.2 for the United States. (The Netherlands, using high fertilizer inputs, regularly averages close to 50 quintals per hectare, the highest yield in the world although no higher than some individual U.S. farmers obtain.)

Farmers in Kansas, the biggest wheat-producing state, use sophisticated knowledge of effective fertilizer application, better soil management practices, summer fallow methods, improved combines, and less waste to raise more than 50 percent more wheat than they did years ago. And they do it on smaller acreage.

Much of the credit for the yield increase belongs to Scout, an improved wheat variety descended from Turkey Red. Scout resists stem rust, leaf rust, smut, and other plant diseases; it develops big heads of grain without lodging (falling over of its own weight) so it can be harvested with efficient combines; it matures early, an important consideration when varieties that mature just two or three days later may be lost to hailstones. (To be cut with a combine, wheat must be dead ripe; grains with moisture content of more than 14 percent must be dried artificially before they can be stored safely). Scout also produces a yield of flour that satisfies millers, and the flour has the characteristics looked for by bakers. So much of the wheat the Russians bought in the summer of 1972 was grown from Scout, whose forebears had come from Russia a century earlier.

Higher-yielding varieties such as Scout, like heavier inputs of fertilizer and pesticides, can serve as substitutes for more land. But as available croplands shrink and populations grow, the world may need more than Scout to avoid the apocalypse of famine.

Looking into the future, many experts see world

populations multiplying; they see hybrid wheat as the only hope for meeting the food crisis.

In the states of Washington and Oregon, where the semidwarf Gaines and Nugaines white wheat varieties are popular, an acre commonly yields fifty to sixty bushels of wheat, nearly twice the average in states such as Kansas where hard red wheat is the big crop.

The high-yielding semidwarf varieties are not hybrids. Hybridization has worked miracles in corn (maize); corn farmers now make well over 100 bushels grow on an acre that once produced only twenty-five bushels. But wheat hybrids are still in the developmental stage, and nobody has developed a satisfactory soybean hybrid.

U.S. soybean yields have more than doubled since 1930, from thirteen bushels per acre to nearly twenty-eight, but other crops have much higher yields and U.S. agronomists dream of a hybrid that could do for soybeans what hybridization has done for corn.

Speaking about soybeans in Columbus, Ohio, in mid-August, 1972, Agriculture Secretary Earl Butz pointed out that it had been forty years since America obtained soybean varieties "from the original home of the soybean." Hailing the progress President Nixon had made in opening up relations with mainland China, Butz ventured a cautious prediction.

"It is not inconceivable," he said, "that as the bamboo curtain opens a bit wider, some day it may be possible for American scientists to seek higher-yielding soybean strains from mainland China."

The Agricultural Research Service, he promised, would send a plant geneticist to Japan and Korea to collect strains of cultivated soybeans and related species in the continuing quest for a key to the yield breakthrough.

Soybeans produce both an oil and a meal; the chief

use of soybean meal is in livestock feed, where it provides far more protein than does corn or other feed grain.

The chief use of wheat of is in human consumption, but although higher-yielding varieties of wheat have been developed, and an acre of land can now produce a lot more wheat than soybeans, a commercially viable wheat hybrid has eluded plant geneticists. It is always just beyond the horizon.

Also beyond that horizon is a world population of 7 billion. To feed such numbers, hybrid wheat may not only be economically desirable but a necessity for human survival. A USDA wheat expert, Louis Reitz, has been quoted as saying that unless hybrid wheats are developed, "I can't help but have a totally dismal outlook for the world's food supply prospects beyond the year 2000."

If a hybrid could do for wheat what hybridization has done for corn, the United States would have even a greater competitive advantage in wheat production than it now has. Since raising U.S. wheat-growing efficiency would protect the export market, the big Minneapolis grain company, Cargill, Inc., is one of the major firms trying to develop hybrid wheat.

Cargill has an additional stake: if the effort succeeds, wheat farmers would no longer be able to save part of their harvest for use as seed, as those Mennonite immigrants to Kansas did a century ago and modern wheat farmers continue to do; they would have to buy new seed each year, as corn farmers do. And the seed company with the miracle hybrid would be in the catbird seat.

Cargill has been an important seed grower for years. If it came up with a hybrid wheat seed, just to grow enough for the U.S. market would require a million acres —an area larger than Rhode Island. Under a 1970 federal law, the seed would be protected against imitation; but such protection is hardly necessary—cracking the formula of a hybrid seed is considered a practical impossibility.

Stealing a hybrid plant is something else again, and the experimental farm that Cargill operates at Fort Collins, Colorado, is a frequent target of industrial espionage. For Cargill is not alone in the race to find a commercial wheat hybrid. Among the other U.S. companies investing millions of dollars in hybridization research are DeKalb Ag-Research, Inc., of DeKalb, Illinois; Hi-Bred Corn Co., of Princeton, Illinois; Funk Bros. Seed Co. of Bloomington, Illinois, and Northrup, King & Co., of Minneapolis. Foreign companies may also be working on hybridization.

And quite probably the Russians as well. In the 1920s the U.S.S.R. was a world leader in the science of plant and animal genetics. But the brilliant Nikolay Ivanovich Vavilov was arrested in 1940 and imprisoned in a windowless underground cell. Despite his mysterious disappearance from world science, at the end of 1942 Vavilov was elected a foreign member of the Royal Society of London, but by then he was so malnourished nothing could save him.

Vavilov's crime was his opposition to Trofim D. Lysenko who, incredibly, dominated agricultural science in the U.S.S.R. from 1934 to 1964. Lysenko substituted Marxist dialectic for objective science, rejecting Darwinism and classical Mendelian laws of genetics. He resisted hybridization and called the chromosome theory of genetics reactionary, idealistic, metaphysical, barren. In its place he proposed intravarietal crossings to renew pureline varieties of self-fertilizing plants. The Soviet biologist Zhores A. Medvedev has called this approach to achieving hybrid vigor "as unlikely as an increase in the amount of water in a corked bottle by shaking it."

But few people dared to question Lysenko in his heyday. Just as modern "organiculturists" say that anyone who doubts them must be a running dog of the chemical fertilizer and pesticide interests, Lysenko called his critics Trotskyite bandits and enemies of the state. Stalin, hearing Lysenko speak in 1935, said, "Bravo, comrade Lysenko, bravo." And when Stalin died Lysenkoism was supported by Khrushchev, whose downfall came about largely through crop failures that might have been averted had he heeded more responsible agronomists.

Russia did have sound men. Pryanishnikov in the 1930s had urged intensifying agriculture with Western European methods of crop rotation and chemical fertilizers. Developing a fertilizer industry was important to national defense, he pointed out, since the manufacture of nitrates and explosives is based on the same technology. But Lysenko listened, instead, to those who claimed that yields could be increased tenfold simply by rotating legumes and cereal grasses, who mixed clover with timothy and cereal grasses (which reduced the clover's nitrogen-fixing effects), and who extolled the supposed virtues of "vernalization." Soaking seeds in water until they swelled, said vernalization enthusiasts, shortened their germination period and protected crops from drought; in practice it proved to be a crackpot idea, as were so many of the ideas put forward by Trofim Denisovich Lysenko.

Lysenko still sits in the prestigious Soviet Academy of Sciences, founded by Peter the Great in 1725; he still receives his lifetime stipend of 500 rubles ($600) a month, four times the average worker's salary; and he has use of chauffeur-driven academy cars and access to special shops closed to ordinary citizens. But Lysenko's doctrines have now been recognized as absurd, and he is reportedly avoided by his fellow academicians.

Brezhnev and Kosygin put an end to the Lysenko follies, and while Zhores Medvedev was forcibly detained in a Soviet mental hospital in 1970 and permitted to leave the country for London early in 1973, possibly as an exile, Russia has returned to the world of scientific reality. Soviet geneticists are almost certainly exploring the possibilities of hybrid wheat varieties that could save the U.S.S.R. from having to sell gold in the future to buy U.S. wheat. The Russians are also moving to improve fertilizer production, which has increased tenfold in the past twenty years but still includes a large percentage of simple fertilizer whose low nutrient content has limited effect on crop yields. In mid-April, 1973, Lenin's old friend Armand Hammer, chairman of Occidental Petroleum, flew home from Moscow in his private Gulfstream II jet with a twenty-year multibillion-dollar agreement that would benefit Soviet fertilizer output. Occidental would supply the U.S.S.R. with technology, equipment, and U.S. superphosphoric acid; it would receive in exchange Soviet-made liquid ammonia, urea, and potash to be marketed in the West.

The Kremlin has reason to agree with the man quoted by Jonathan Swift in *Gulliver's Travels*, the man who "gave it for his opinion that whoever could make two ears of corn, or two blades of grass, to grow upon a spot of ground where only one grew before, would deserve better of mankind, and do more essential service to his country, than the whole race of politicians put together."

To Swift, "corn" meant grain, any grain. Until a man could make two ears, two heads, two bushels, two quintals of grain grow where only one grew before, the specter of starvation would increasingly stalk the world as populations multiplied and arable land diminished.

17.

In the spring and summer of 1973, Exportkhleb was again playing the role of "Importkhleb." Other longtime wheat exporters like Argentina and Australia were still being plagued with drought and had to turn down customers. China and India, as well as the Soviet Union, were looking to North America as the only substantial source of grain, but now there were no carryover reserves of wheat in U.S. and Canadian bins; export demand was keeping prices far above 1972 levels, and unfavorable weather at home or abroad could send them through the roof.

Were predictions of world famine that far-fetched?

If the United States were to raise more wheat for export and still have enough to keep domestic prices in hand, American farmers would obviously have to plant more acres, use more fertilizer, or find higher-yielding varieties.

But in a free economy the government could not order farmers to plant more wheat, it could only encourage them to do so.

Of America's roughly 350 million acres of farmland.
about 60 million have been set-aside acres; another 50
million or so have in recent years been planted in wheat.
(Soviet wheat acreage is more than three times that, but
the Soviet wheat crop is at best only about twice the U.S.
crop.) In the late 1940s and '50s, U.S. wheat acreage was
a third again as large as today, and the decline is attribu-
table in part to the fact that about 15 million acres have
been taken out of wheat production.

Most wheat farmers participated in the USDA's voluntary diversion program that sets aside land that might
otherwise be planted in wheat. The program was still in
effect in the fall of 1972, but it was not being pushed.

"Now that the price of wheat has gone up by 50 cents
to 60 cents a bushel," said Earl Butz in early September,
"we're pretty confident farmers will use their pencils and
figure, and we won't get the participation we earlier hoped
to get. In fact, we don't want the participation we earlier
hoped to get."

He was counting on high wheat prices to make farmers forgo subsidy and plant all the wheat they wanted.
Farmers would be left to make their own choice, but "I
think we'll get relatively low participation in the set aside
and I hope we do."

Butz was wrong. When planting figure were released
in mid-December, it turned out that farmers had planted
just over 1 percent more land in wheat instead of at least
10 percent more as expected. Fertilizer purchases were
up, and it looked as if the 1973 crop might top the record
1971 figure, but not by any fat margin.

U.S. wheat farmers netted about $3.4 billion in 1972,
up some $350 million from the year before and $300 million above the previous high set in 1947. Had they taken
their pencils and figured that overproduction would lower

prices and reduce their incomes? Not likely. Wheat farmers are among the last individualists. While some large
fruit and vegetable growers may be in positions to influence prices of their crops, no single wheat farmer is big
enough to carry much clout in the marketplace, and no
alliance has ever united many farmers to limit production.
Eternally optimistic, farmers tend to grow as much as they
can. Wet fields prevented fall planting in some Midwestern states, and in some Plains states winter wheat planting
was up 5 or 6 percent; but it looked as if wheat farmers
might be planting very nearly as much wheat as they
could, diversion program or no diversion program.

Said Assistant Secretary Carroll Brunthaver: "We
may be closer to full production capacity in wheat than
we realize."

If America could grow only 44 million tons or so of
wheat, it could hardly feed the world and meet all its own
needs as well, not without wheat prices going sky-high.

Political considerations had certainly been a factor in
restraining the USDA from pushing too hard earlier for
crop increases. After the 1970 southern corn blight, which
destroyed 15 percent of the U.S. corn harvest and helped
boost meat prices by raising the price of feed grain, Earl
Butz's predecessor Clifford Hardin had allowed farmers to
use up to 20 percent more of their corn-growing land that
would otherwise have lain fallow. Corn plantings increased
by almost 7 million acres, to 64 million, and when corn
prices sank the following year, farmers in the Corn Belt
demanded Hardin's head.

Orville Freeman, Hardin's predecessor who said he
could not err on the side of too little grain when India
and Pakistan were threatened with starvation, had been
the farmers' target when Freeman's high 1967 output
goals pushed farm prices down.

Republicans in the fall of 1972 were not about to alienate farmers, even if it meant an inadequate wheat crop. Farm state votes had given Richard Nixon his slim election victory margin in 1968.

Only when the 1972 elections were safely in the bag did the Nixon administration finally act to reduce pressures on wheat prices. The USDA announced in December that farm and warehouse loans on stored grain would not be extended. Farmers who had been holding wheat from past harvests under government loans, gambling that prices would go up, would now have to sell. This would force an estimated 6½ million tons into the market. In January, the Commodity Credit Corporation was ordered to dispose of all grain stocks "except for small quantities of emergency reserves." The CCC in fact abdicated its responsibility to maintain reserves, and by April it owned virtually no grain at all.

Turning loose the reserves probably created as many problems as it solved. Farmers with bins full of wheat (some had 40,000 to 60,000 bushels in storage) loaded up their trucks and converged on country grain elevators. But grain elevators throughout the wheat belts were backed up with wheat they were unable to move for lack of rail-cars.

"It all boils down to moving three or four years' crops in one year," said a Burlington Northern official. His railroad had ordered 1,000 new hopper cars for summer delivery, but he said "the railroad pipeline to the Gulf ports is full and is going to stay full through December of 1973 and probably through the first half of 1974. With the CCC calling in grain which has been stored all the way back to 1968, and with the great 1972 crop on top of that, well, there's just too much stuff."

Soon the winter wheat would be greening. Farmers were told they would be allowed to harvest some 800,000 acres of winter wheat they would otherwise have had to plow under to meet conservation requirements. And Treasury Secretary Shultz ordered the elimination of the required set aside for wheat, permitting production of up to 1.9 million tons of additional spring wheat. Don Paarlberg, the USDA's ranking economist, told a reporter that these steps were mostly "useless." But, he added, there really were "damn few things" that could be done.

Early in 1973 U.S. television viewers saw a face not often seen on the screen when Bill D. Moyers interviewed George F. Kennan, who had served as U.S. ambassador to Moscow in Russia's days of terror under Josef Stalin.

Kennan recalled that the Russians had constantly challenged his faith in America, saying that everybody under capitalism was out for himself, with no common spirit or dream, no national aspiration. Listening to the bitterness and cynicism voiced in New York City today, said Kennan, he felt America was in deep trouble.

The Soviet Union shares America's dilemma of ethnic heterogeneity; the Russians have been able to maintain their Union only through autocratic rule. And even that autocracy has had to recognize and respond to consumer demand.

More Spartanly self-denying have been the racially homogeneous masses of Maoist China. Khrushchev called China a beggars' communism, "a state of poverty at the subsistence level elevated into a principle, with poverty defined as virtue so as to prevent any dangerous striving for consumer goods from raising its head."

Peking, in turn, has accused Moscow of backsliding from the pure ideals of Marxism in appeasing the bourgeois demands of the people. China, according to the joke, has graduated from destitution to poverty. But the

Chinese people—one fourth of mankind—has for the first time in history been unified. It has been imbued with a national sense of purpose, a national dignity, a powerful motivation to modernize its ancient ways.

In terms of providing its people with the necessities and even luxuries of life, America stands in sharp contrast to China and Russia. In those terms it is hardly in what George Kennan called "deep trouble." But a diplomat thinks inevitably in terms of national power. And Kennan may have been remembering what Richard Nixon had said in his State of the Union message in 1972:

"I think of what happened to Greece and Rome and you see what is left—only the pillars. What has happened, of course, is that great civilizations of the past, as they have become wealthy, as they have lost their will to live, to improve, they then have become subject to the decadence that eventually destroys the civilization. The U.S. is now reaching that point . . ."

In 1972 America's Food for Peace was wheat. But wheat can also be food for war. When it chose sides in the brief, bloody war between India and Pakistan, the United States—or at least its President—sided with Pakistan and thus with China.

If war loomed between China and the U.S.S.R.—and there were always rumors that Moscow contemplated a preventive strike against Chinese nuclear capability—would the United States give preference to the Chinese? Would Chinese troops be provisioned with U.S. wheat?

Moscow neatly forestalled that possibility when it sent Belousov, Kalitenko, and Sakun to Washington and New York in the summer of 1972. The decision as to who would receive U.S. grain was taken out of Washington's hands as Moscow turned the free market system against America and employed it to serve the national interests of Russia. U.S. foreign policy *was*, in effect, made by Continental, Cargill, and the other private trading companies, much in the way the East India Company once dictated British foreign policy. Longshoremen were not the only Metternichs.

If Moscow's ploy was to keep China from buying America's wheat, then Peking would have to learn of the Russian buying. That is where John Smith would come in. Morton Sosland's mysterious informant made his initial calls only after the Belousov group had bought practically all the grain it originally intended to buy. When Smith telephoned again on July 31, his report of the Russians' return to buy more grain risked boosting the price Moscow would have to pay. But the Russians are as adept at contract bridge as they are at chess: a preemptive bid for U.S. grain may have been deemed so valuable that it justified a somewhat higher price. Moscow may have counted on Peking's reluctance to lose face just as much as it counted on the capitalist system to keep the early deals quiet while it beat Peking to the punch.

Admittedly this is speculation; unless Mr. Smith surfaces and tells all, his motives will remain obscure. Perhaps, after all, the Russians bought no more grain in 1972 than they actually needed. Were 1973 Soviet purchases motivated by similar genuine internal needs or by dog in the manger strategy? The issue will long be argued. Nikolai Belousov's anxious return visit in early 1973 to expedite shipments will be cited to prove Russia's urgent need, and to discredit suggestions that anything more was involved in 1972 than buying American grain at a tremendous bargain.

It turned out to be an even bigger bargain than the Russians knew. For in February, 1973, on Lincoln's Birthday, Treasury Secretary George Shultz announced another devaluation of the U.S. dollar. Moscow could now buy dollars at a 10 percent reduction. And since the Soviets had thus far paid only $330 to $400 million for their grain, buying the rest on credit under the terms announced July 8th, Moscow stood to reap a windfall saving.

Some 4.9 million tons of wheat had been shipped by February 12, and the Russians had used up $126.5 million worth of credit to buy that wheat. Add $55.9 million worth of credit they had used to buy 1.1 million tons of corn, and the CCC had disbursed a total of $182.4 million to the export companies to pay for grain the Russians had bought on the cuff. In addition, the export companies had registered additional amounts of Russian grain for CCC payments to be made when the grain left port: $241.9 million for wheat, $4.3 million for corn, and $21.5 million for rye—a total of $267.7 million. The upper limit of credit that could be outstanding in any one year under the agreement was $500 million.

By March 16, another $67.6 million worth of grain had left port and the CCC had disbursed a total of $250 million to pay the export companies for their Russian grain shipments: $177.5 million for wheat, $72.3 million for corn. On top of that, the CCC had outstanding registrations from the export companies of another $250 million to be paid when grain shipments left port: $201 million for wheat, $27.9 million for corn, and the $21.5 million for the rye that had not yet been shipped.

Of the $500 million in credit used by the Russians, $317.6 million was disbursed after devaluation. Repayment of all $500 million would be in devalued dollars.

The credit terms, as it worked out, gave the Russians what amounted to a "call" option on devaluation; when the dollar was in fact devalued on February 12, it meant a saving of $80 to $87 million for Moscow. It meant that most of the wheat the Russians bought had cost them not $60 a ton but only $54, a mere $1.48 a bushel.

The Russians, moreover, were getting fantastic prices

for the $2 billion in gold they were selling. Supported by monetary authorities at $35 an ounce until 1968, gold had gone up as the dollar weakened. On February 12, devaluation day, gold bullion sold in the London market at about $68 an ounce, just below the $70 mark it had hit August 1. Within two weeks, as confidence in the U.S. dollar weakened, gold bullion touched $95 an ounce; the head of the gold trading department at a large Swiss bank said gold would be over $100 an ounce (as it later was) were it not for supplies of the precious metal coming in from the Soviet Union.

Gold, as the legendary King Midas discovered, is not edible, but in 1973 gold was helping Moscow beat the high cost of eating.

Of the $54 billion in gold held by the world governments, including the International Monetary Fund, Russia held almost $4 billion, less than 8 percent. In 1952 the U.S.S.R. had held $5 billion in gold, over 10 percent of the then $48.2 billion total. The United States in 1952 had held $28 billion worth of gold, 58 percent of the world total, and Britain $2.2 billion. As Russia's share dropped by more than $1 billion in the next twenty years, Britain's gold hoard dwindled to $900 million. And the U.S. supply fell by more than half to $11.7 billion, about 22 percent of the world total. The International Fund ($6.4 billion), West Germany ($5 billion), France ($4.3 billion), Switzerland, and Italy (3.5 billion each) increased their gold holdings dramatically. (Figures are based on a price of $42.22 per ounce; totals refer only to government-held gold and ignore private holdings, especially big in the oil-rich Middle East.)

Moscow in early 1973 was selling gold—as much gold as the U.S.S.R. mines in three years—to pay for the bargain grain it had bought from the West. And the high price of gold made that grain an even bigger bargain.

When Exportkhleb first bought grain in the summer of 1972, gold was fetching less than $60 an ounce; it took more than an ounce of gold to buy a ton of U.S. wheat. In the early months of 1973 an ounce of gold paid for 1.3 tons of wheat bought earlier on credit at $60 a ton. The high price of gold, together with the explicit devaluation of the dollar, brought Moscow's price for U.S. wheat down below $1 a bushel.

For U.S. food prices, devaluation had a less happy significance. It meant for one thing that U.S. food commodities like beef, eggs, feed grains, pork, poultry, and wheat would be cheaper in terms of the franc, the mark, the lira, the ruble, the yen, and other foreign currency. Instead of taking 5.6 francs to buy a dollar's worth as it had in 1971, it now took only 4.6. It took 2.9 deutschmarks instead of 3.7, 572 liras instead of 625, .75 rubles instead of .83, 264 yen instead of 360. And there were no meat price ceilings in some other countries as there were in the United States. Higher export demand could be anticipated, with a further shrinking of supplies available for domestic tables.

While the United States imports far more meat than it exports, the nation did export 42 million pounds of beef in 1971 and 52 million in 1972; in 1973 it would export at least 70 million pounds, much of it in nutritious organ meats (brains, hearts, kidneys, livers, and such that Americans tend to scorn), and possibly a good deal more. Export markets would also take great tonnages of U.S. wheat, soybeans, and feed grains.

Foods America imports—bananas, many cheeses, cocoa, coffee, most fish, some meat, spices, sugar, tea, and a variety of specialty items—would be more expensive.

18.

Three days after the 1973 dollar devaluation, Richard Nixon made a radio address on matters of environment and natural resources. He had just named his agriculture secretary "Counselor on Natural Resources," and the President justified that by saying, "One of the most precious natural resources since our earliest days has been American agriculture."

He had little new to say about the environment, but the President made headlines by coming out on the side of the USDA committee report urging an end to farm subsidies.

In some other year a proposal to phase out government farm controls would have faced almost certain defeat, but high prices of wheat and other commodities, bid up in large part as a result of the huge Soviet purchases, had changed the climate of opinion among many farmers as well as consumers.

A White House economist quoted by *The Wall Street Journal* in January had said, "This is the best opportunity we've had in thirty years to fundamentally alter farm programs." Richard Nixon was now seizing the opportunity.

"My administration is not going to express its goal for farmers in confusing terms," said the President. "Our goal, instead, is very simple. The farmer wants, has earned, and deserves more freedom to make his own decisions. The nation wants and needs expanded supplies of reasonably priced goods and commodities."

Henry Wallace's system of acreage allotments to limit the production of major crops was, in Richard Nixon's words, "drastically outdated." So were direct payments to farmers to supplement their incomes from crops, a program begun under Orville Freeman. Under the new Republican plan, the aim would be to reduce the farmer's dependence on government payments for part of his income, to give him more freedom in planting decisions, and to pave the way for increased crop exports.

Exports would save the U.S. farmer from price-depressing surpluses. Farm exports had set records for three straight years; they had amounted to $9 billion worth in 1972 and would easily exceed President Nixon's ambitious goal of $10 billion in the crop year ending June 30, 1973.

Almost nobody defended the subsidy program as it stood. The fiction of "parity prices" was an obvious butt of ridicule. In mid-December, 1972, U.S. farmers were paying prices 4½ times what they had paid in the five years prior to World War I; prices for their farm products were 3½ times what they had been then. Wheat prices, on a national average, were at 76 percent of parity, up from only 45 percent a year earlier.

It would make more sense, said critics of subsidy, to

give poor farmers welfare than to use a subsidy system that both taxed consumers and increased their food costs to support prosperous farmers more than poor ones.

But to abandon government controls and leave farmers to their own devices seemed to many a dubious approach.

Was overproduction really no longer a problem? Some farm economists reminded critics of subsidy of what occurred in 1971, when overplanting of corn after the 1970 blight pushed corn prices in some areas to a point below the cost of production. A free economy works well in theory, and U.S. agriculture is much freer than any other major industry, they said. But farmers are human. They have fancy equipment, fertilizers, and pesticides, and their natural inclination is to use their technology to grow as much as they can whether or not they have a good market. Look what happened to egg prices in your free economy.

Farm exports can reduce our trade deficits and raise our employment levels, these economists said. We should certainly expand trade with Russia and China. But foreign markets have a history of vanishing between planting time and harvest; with export subsidies cut off on farm exports, U.S. farmers are competing with foreign farmers who have low labor costs and are subsidized so they can undercut U.S. prices; if Americans are to compete successfully, they must have some cushion to hedge their risk in producing for export.

It would be folly, the economists said, to chart a course on the basis of one year's experience. The 1972 bubble could burst if Russia, China, and some other countries had good crop years in 1973. Prices would plummet. Both farmers and consumers need some program to protect them against wildly fluctuating prices.

One such program would set up a national food bank,

which would be stocked with $1.5 to $2 billion worth of wheat and feed grains, with the stocks rotated to avoid spoilage. Such a strategic reserve would enable the United States to provide disaster relief at home and abroad, to meet the needs of a civil defense emergency, to relieve hunger among the needy, to support a healthy farm economy, and to spare supermarket customers the pressures of superpower politics. It would cost $200 to $300 million a year in storage costs, and additional millions to pay farmers for surplus crops needed to maintain this ever-normal granary, but the money would come from general tax revenues, not from consumer food budgets.

One month before the President's radio speech about ending farm subsidies, Earl Butz had addressed the Chicago Mercantile Exchange. Price supports, he said, have historically proved to serve as "disappointing" price ceilings rather than effective price floors. A free market, Butz said, was "the best safeguard farmers have against government controls which would no doubt be oriented to cheap food."

For Earl Butz, "cheap food" is a term of opprobrium. American consumers, few of whom are still farmers, do not share his view. And whereas Richard Nixon has held out the promise of "expanded supplies of reasonably priced" commodities as the reward for returning to a free economy, his eagerness to abandon farm controls may have been motivated mainly by a desire to cut government spending.

If farm subsidies served only the farmer, if they worked only to restrict planting, limit production, and keep prices high, there would be a strong case to abandon them. But even with subsidies, farmers have probably been planting very nearly as much wheat as they would have planted anyway. Only just so much land is suitable for growing wheat. Not even the highest wheat prices in twenty years persuaded farmers to increase their winter wheat acreage by more than a niggardly 1 percent in the fall of 1972.

Not only Americans, but Britons and Japanese have benefited from U.S. subsidies to farmers and exporters, and of American carry-overs in years of surplus that were released in leaner years when prices got too high. Britain and Japan are the world's two leading food importers, and their economic expansion—for a century in Britain's case, for twenty years in Japan's—has been based on government policies of cheap food.

Early in 1973, the chairman of Cadbury Schweppes in England stated that "the era of cheap food is over."

Lord Watkinson was talking about more than the entry of Britain into Europe's Common Market. And his words had significance for Americans and Japanese as well as for Britons.

It is inflationary to pump tax money into the economy, but higher food prices are also inflationary; they are, in fact, the edge of inflation that cuts most cruelly into those least able to afford it. If tax money is used to supplement the farmer's income, he is supported equitably by all taxpayers (now that there is no bread tax), according to their means. If the farmer's income is maintained with high commodity prices, then the poor, who must spend a larger share of their incomes for food, bear the chief burden of supporting the farmer.

Farm subsidies have in practice benefited rich farmers and put poor ones out of business. When some farmers receive upwards of $100,000 each in tax money, farm subsidies offend everyone's sense of justice. But subsidies have in fact kept U.S. farmers producing food in abundance, both for domestic use and for normal export sale, at prices often barely equal to the cost of production.

To expect export markets to replace federal price supports as an incentive to farming assumes several things:

1. That the Russian and Chinese buying in 1972 was the result of something more than freak weather conditions in so many countries that normally produce grain surpluses.

2. That whatever else motivated such heavy foreign buying will continue.

3. That U.S. relations with the Communist powers will remain as harmonious as they were in 1972.

4. That Japan will continue to be the major customer for U.S. meat, milk, eggs, wheat, and feed grains it has been in the past.

5. That the U.S.S.R. and Eastern Europe will maintain their policies of upgrading their diets to include more animal protein.

6. That U.S. labor will stay on the job and give export customers no reason to doubt America's ability to deliver consistently on its contracts.

7. That U.S. grain elevators, railroads, and port facilities will have the capacity to expedite shipments of export commodities.

8. And that U.S. farmers will have the incentive of continued high prices to maintain their high rates of production.

A lot of assumptions there. And the last one will stick in consumers' throats.

When Lord Watkinson spoke of "cheap food," he was thinking of prices even higher in terms of income than the food prices that Americans were complaining about. For although it is misleading to say, as Earl Butz has done, that Americans pay less than 16 cents of their after-tax dollars for food, it is true that per capita income in the United States went up 62 percent from 1965 to 1972, while food prices went up only 33 percent. And Butz's 16 percent figure does serve at least for comparison with other countries. Britons, in "the era of cheap food," spent about 25 percent of their disposable income on food; Japanese spent 35 percent; Italians and Greeks spent more; and the average Pole or Russian spent half his income or more to feed his family on a diet skimpier than the austerity diets that "high prices" were imposing on many Americans.

Food prices went up throughout the world in 1973; the "grain drain" lamented by hard-pressed U.S. housewives worked greater hardships overseas than it did in America. This was small consolation. Nor was there much comfort in being told that Americans probably contributed more to world harmony by paying higher food prices than by spending tax dollars on "defense" appropriations.

To let the people of Russia, China, India, or of any other country go hungry while Americans got fat would scarcely serve the family of nations. Whether Americans would willingly pay more for their food in order to relieve hunger abroad is another question. Anyway, was it fair to ask the poor of America to bear more than their share of the humanitarian effort?

It might be argued that supermarket prices were driven up by powers beyond human control, powers bigger than superpower politics. But much of the world's crop failure came from money being spent on weaponry instead of husbandry, on arms instead of farms, on ammunition instead of irrigation.

If the 1972 grain deals represented a commercial Russian food relief program, America's part in it was largely unintentional. It is well that we exported so much grain—well for the future of East-West relations, well for our balance of trade; it is splendid that we were in a position to do it. But we did not so much do it ourselves as have it done for us, without our knowledge, despite our possible objections; and there is no denying the fact that it was done in a way that put an unfair burden on those who spend such a large part of their after-tax incomes at the supermarket.

Supermarket patrons in 1973—beefing, crabbing, grousing, bellyaching about food prices, boycotting meat —looked for scapegoats.

Some directed their wrath at the grocers, but all the evidence indicated that supermarket profit margins were, if anything, smaller than ever. Retailers were hurting as much as their customers were.

Some customers blamed the farmers, who were now getting good prices after so many years of being squeezed off the land by rising costs; but the farmers' share of the food dollar was not much higher than it had always been.

Labor unions came in for criticism, but hourly wages of farm workers, meat cutters, bakery truck drivers, retail grocery clerks, and other food industry employees were not excessive when compared with wages in other industries.

Federal farm programs and policies that restricted production were lambasted, but when farmers have overproduced one year they have generally underproduced the next; low prices have been followed by high prices; in the long run, a free boom-bust cycle would benefit neither farmers nor consumers.

Agriculture Secretary Earl Butz blamed consumers themselves for hiking the price of food, which he insisted was still a bargain considering how much money Americans had to spend. It was not high costs that were *pushing* up food prices, he said, it was insatiable consumer demand that was *pulling* them up. But while demand had indeed risen, Butz admitted that rising feed costs discouraged farmers from raising more cattle, hogs, and poultry.

No one could deny that extraordinary export demand had been the major factor in boosting the cost of wheat, feed grains, and soybeans. For lack of ample granary reserves, in the absence of any export licenses or quotas, meeting the export demand meant upsetting the price equilibrium of those commodities, creating the biggest logistics foulup in the nation's history, and triggering a chain of price jumps that ended at supermarket checkout counters.

Putting the finger on exports caused some fingers to be pointed at the big private export houses, which had sold so much grain to the Soviet Union in 1972, and at the U.S. Department of Agriculture, which had done nothing to control the large exports except to encourage them with subsidies.

Democrats accused the USDA of playing footsie with the export companies, and charged the FBI and Justice Department with covering up information that might embarrass the Nixon administration. Republicans said the charges were simply political mudslinging.

It was all beside the point. Whether or not there were improprieties in the sales made to Exportkhleb (and the outcries came mostly from farmers who had sold their crops before prices went up), the Americans who did the selling acted as any other American businessmen would have done. They undertook certain risks in the expectation of gaining profits; they had legitimate reason to believe that their sales would create more jobs in America, ease the nation's trade deficit, and help relax tensions between East and West. Carroll Brunthaver no doubt acted with the same high motives, and with the added incentive of helping U.S. wheat growers.

What none of these gentlemen fully appreciated was
the effect the sales would have in igniting a chain of fire-
crackers. At the end of the chain was the supermarket
checkout counter, and the prices they paid at that counter
in 1973 made many Americans, justly or unjustly, feel as
warmly toward Richard Nixon as Soviet citizens had felt
toward Nikita Khrushchev ten years earlier.

And how did Mr. Nixon feel about the Russian grain
deals? He coined a word:

Said the President of the United States, "We were
schnookered."

Bobby Fischer might have used a chess term: the
President was "forked." He was in a position to lose
either his farm support or his consumer support; one was
inevitably lost, and Richard Nixon could no longer
equivocate.

Those who were "schnookered" most by the Soviet
grain deals were the little people of America, and of the
world, who had been pawns of superpower strategy at a
bargaining table at the New York Hilton.

Food prices in America reflected the shrewd buying
of Nikolai Belousov; the artful, well-intentioned salesman-
ship of Michel Fribourg, Barney Saunders, Ned Cook,
and the others; the blind eye of Carroll Brunthaver; and
the laissez-faire system of free enterprise that was giving
America, for all its booming peacetime economy, a taste
of wartime deprivation.

While Nixon inflation-fighters insisted that the situation was temporary, there was a growing suspicion in
the land that "the era of cheap food" was indeed forever
over.

"The world is moving through a true watershed in
food production and demand," Morton Sosland declared
in *The New York Times*. "This is an economic develop-

ment of historic importance, all too little appreciated and most dangerous to neglect."

Supermarket prices might never again be the same. Their new plateau rested on the history-making deals pulled off by Russian purchasing agents, and on new farm policies made possible only by those colossal secret deals the mysterious John Smith kept trying to reveal.

For many Americans, certainly to the 36 million living below the poverty line, higher food prices were as frightening as any bread, potato, or rice shortages in wartime Russia or China. AT&T, CBS, IBM, RCA, and General Motors could all go out of business tomorrow and the country would survive, but we cannot do without food. We all have to eat. And how well we eat depends on what we can afford.

Perhaps never before in recent American history has the delicate balance between food supplies and food prices been brought home so clearly and harshly as it was in 1973. From farm to feedlot to railhead to packing plant to mill to bakery to shipping dock to supermarket, we saw how a marginal change in the supply-demand ratio could set off a volatile chain reaction that hurt us where we lived.

We were forced to take another look at our supposedly bottomless cornucopia of field and fruited plain, and what we saw made us less smug. Many of us would henceforth keep an eye on crop conditions and harvests with a concern once felt only by commodity speculators.

As for the immediate future, all the spilt milk scrambling to patch things up, all the jawboning, all the wage-price freezes, and all the consumer boycotts could not change the fact that the vital essential of life had been thrown into chaos beginning on the day some Russians came to New York to buy American grain.

SELECTED SOURCES

CHAPTER 1

Isadore Barmash, *The New York Times,* February 14, 1973; Edward Cowan, *The New York Times,* February 22, 1973; Phil Gailey, *The Washington Post,* March 28, 1972; Michael C. Jensen, *The New York Times,* February 23, 1973; Peter Milius, *The Washington Post,* January 10 and March 22, 1973; Sylvia Porter column, August 17, 1972; William Robbins, *The New York Times,* February 21 and March 25, 1973.

CHAPTER 2

Bruce Davidson, *The Boston Globe,* October 22, 1972; John Fialka, *The Washington Evening Star,* October 29 and 30, 1972.

USDA figures. Russell Lord, *The Care of the Earth,* New York: Mentor, 1963.

USDA figures. Robert Keatley, *The Wall Street Journal,* April 10, 1973; Nick Kotz, *The Washington Post,* October 8, 1972; Harrison Salisbury, *Russia,* New York: Atheneum, 1972.

E. W. Kenworthy, *The New York Times,* March 26, 1973; Reuters News Service; *Sale of Wheat to Russia:* hearings before the Subcommittee on Livestock and Grains of the House Agriculture Committee, September 14, 18, and 19, 1972, U.S. Government Printing Office, Serial No. 92-KK; interview with Morton I. Sosland; Michael Tatu, *Power in the Kremlin: From Khrushchev to Kosygin,* New York: Viking Compass, 1970.

The New York Times 1963–64, stories and editorial; Harrison Salisbury, op. cit.; interviews with Edward Kimmel, Bureau of International Commerce, Department of Commerce, with Frederick Larsen, U.S. Maritime Administration, Department of Commerce, and with Morton I. Sosland.

CHAPTER 3

Interviews with Sheldon L. Berens, Continental Grain Co. and with James Bowe of Carl Byoir & Associates attached to Cargill, Inc.; *Business Week,* March 11, 1972; *The New York Times,* January 12, 1964; *Time,* October 18, 1963.

Tom BeVier, *Memphis Commercial Appeal,* October 15, 1972; *Sale of Wheat to Russia:* hearings, 1972, op. cit.; interviews with Edward W. Cook of Cook Industries, Inc., with Michael C. Jensen, with John A. Schnittker, and with Morton I. Sosland.

E. W. Kenworthy, *The New York Times,* op. cit., *The Washington Post,* March 21, 1973; *Sale of Wheat to Russia:* hearings, 1972, op. cit.; interviews with USDA staff people, with Sheldon L. Berens, and with Morton I. Sosland.

CHAPTER 4

Interviews with Nelson Chang and Morris J. Markovitz of Hayden, Stone, Inc.; *Business Week,* December 23, 1972; Elizabeth Fowler, *The New York Times,* September 12 and November 13, 1972, and January 7, 1973; H. J. Maidenberg, *The New York Times,* March 15, 1973; Robert J. Samuelson, *The Washington Post,* December 16, 1972; "Adam Smith," *Supermoney,* New York: Random House, 1972; *Time,* April 2, 1973.

Bruce Davidson, *The Boston Globe,* op. cit.; *Sale of Wheat to Russia:* hearings, 1972, op. cit.; Reuters News Service; interviews with John A. Schnittker and with Morton I. Sosland; U.P.I., November 4, 1972.

Tom BeVier, *Memphis Commercial Appeal,* op. cit.; interviews with Edward W. Cook, with Philip A. McCaull of Louis Dreyfus Corporation, and with W. B. Saunders of Cargill, Inc., *Sale of Wheat to Russia:* hearings, 1972, op. cit.

Tom BeVier, *Memphis Commercial Appeal,* op. cit.; *Sale of Wheat to Russia:* hearings, 1972, op. cit.; interviews with Edward W. Cook and W. B. Saunders.

CHAPTER 5

Nick Kotz, *The Washington Post,* October 21, 1972; *Milling & Baking News,* October 3, 1972; interview with Morton I. Sosland.

Barron's, August 14, 1972; *The New York Times,* early August, 1972.

Sale of Wheat to Russia: hearings, 1972, op. cit.; *The New York Times* stories; interviews with Thomas Connally of Cargill, Inc., with Philip A. McCaull, and with W. B. Saunders.

Milling & Baking News, op. cit.; Reuters News Service; *The Southwestern Miller,* August 2, 1972; interview with Morton I. Sosland; *Sale of Wheat to Russia:* hearings, 1972, op. cit.

Tom BeVier, *Memphis Commercial Appeal,* op. cit.; H. J. Maidenberg, *The New York Times,* August 12, 1972; interviews with Edward W. Cook and John A. Schnittker; Tad Szulc, *The New York Times,* November 18, 1972; Neil Ulman, *The Wall Street Journal,* January 23, 1973.

Interviews with James Bowe and Morton I. Sosland; *Milling & Baking News,* op. cit.

Business Week, March 11, 1972; *Milling & Baking News,* op. cit.; interviews with James Bowe, Morton I. Sosland, and others.

CHAPTER 6

G. L. Carefoot and E. R. Sprott, *Famine on the Wind,* New York: Rand McNally, 1967; John G. Fuller, *The Day of St. Anthony's Fire,* New York: Macmillan, 1968; James Trager, *The Bellybook,* New York: Grossman, 1972.

John A. Prestbo, *The Wall Street Journal,* November 3, 1972; Reuters News Service, November 3, 1972; *Sale of Wheat to Russia:* hearings, 1972, op. cit.; interviews with Frederick Larsen, John A. Schnittker, and Morton I. Sosland.

Thomas C. Cochran and William Miller, *The Age of Enterprise: A Social History of Industrial America,* New York: Harper Torchbooks, 1965; Evan Jones and the editors of Time-Life Books, *The Plains States,* New York: Time-Life Books, 1968; Federal Writers' Project, *Kansas: A Guide to the Sunflower State,* 2d printing, New York: Hastings House, 1949; Herman Steen in *Milling & Baking News,* January 30, 1973.

Marilyn Berger, *The Washington Post,* November 17, 1972; Frank Crepeau, *New York Post,* December 20, 1972; Robert Eugene Cushman, *Leading Constitutional Decisions,* New York: F. S. Crofts, 1940; Bowen Northrup, *The Wall Street Journal,* January 31, 1973; Tad Szulc, *The New York Times,* November 23, 1972.

CHAPTER 7

Merle Fainsod and Lincoln Gordon, *Government and the American Economy,* New York: W. W. Norton, 1941; Russell Lord, *The Care of the Earth,* op. cit.

B. Drummond Ayres, *The New York Times,* December 5, 1971; David P. Garino, *The Wall Street Journal,* January 31, 1973; Spencer Rich, *The Washington Post,* March 19, 1973; Herman Steen, *The Southwestern Miller,* September 26, 1972.

Interviews with Charles W. Cobb, Claude Freeman, and James J. Naive, Economic Research Service, U.S. Department of Agriculture, with John A. Schnittker, and with Morton I. Sosland.

Milling & Baking News, January 30, February 6 and 20, and March 6 and 13, 1973.

Interviews with Lawrence O'Brien, ITT-Continental Bakeries, and others.

CHAPTER 8

Raymond R. Anderson, *The New York Times,* November 1, 1967; Associated Press, February 1, 1973; James Feron, *The New York Times,* October 7, 1971; Harrison Salisbury, *Russia,* op. cit.; Leslie Shabad, *The New York Times,* November 11, 1972; Hedrick Smith, *The New York Times,* September 3, 1972, and February 4, 1973; Raymond A. Sokolov, *The New York Times,* May 4, 1972.

CHAPTER 9

Clark Mollenhoff, James Risser, and George Anthan, *Des Moines Register,* March 18, 19, 20, 21, 22, and 23; Mary Russell, *The Washington Post,* March 16, 1973; interviews with Nelson Chang and Morris J. Markovitz of Hayden, Stone, Inc. and with Chester W. Keltner of Keltner Statistical Service, Kansas City.

Michael C. Jensen, *The New York Times,* October 21, 1972; Don Kendall, AP, *Kansas City Star,* October 20, 1972; Nick Kotz, *The Washington Post,* October 21, 1972; *The Washington Post,* March 9, 1973; interview with Morton I. Sosland.

Tom Braden, *The Washington Post,* November 23, 1971; William R. Doerner, *Time,* February 26, 1973; Julius Duscha, *The New York Times Magazine,* April 16, 1972; Nick Kotz, *The Washington Post,* November 24, 1971; *The New York Times* editorial, December 28, 1971; William Raspberry, *The Washington Post,* November 24, 1971; Burt Schorr, *The Wall Street Journal,* August 21, 1972.

CHAPTER 10

Mary Bralove, Dan Dorfman, Charles J. Elias, and John D. Williams, *The Wall Street Journal,* February 14, 1973; Michael C. Jensen, *The New York Times,* February 23, 1973; Leonard Sloane, *The New York Times,* February 5, 1973; *Supermarket News,* 1972 and 1973; Eleanor

Johnson Tracy, *Fortune,* January, 1973; James Trager, *The Food-book,* New York: Grossman, 1970, Avon, 1972.

Edwin L. Dale, *The New York Times,* January 14, 1973; Norman H. Fischer, *The Wall Street Journal,* June 5, 1972, E. S. E. Hafez, *Reproduction in Farm Animals,* Philadelphia: Lea & Febiger, 1968; Hendrik S. Houthakker, *New Republic,* April 21, 1973; Michael C. Jensen *The New York Times,* June 27, 1972; Stephen Joselik, *The Wall Street Journal,* June 19, 1972; Seth S. King, *The New York Times,* March 23, 1973; Will Lissner, *The New York Times,* March 5, 1973; Richard D. Lyons, *The New York Times,* April 3, 1972; Francis L. Partsch, *The Wall Street Journal,* December 6, 1971; Sylvia Porter column, February 16, 1973; James L. Rowe, Jr., *The Washington Post,* March 18, 1973; Robert J. Samuelson, *The Washington Post,* April 2, 1972; James C. Tanner, *The New York Times,* August 18, 1972; *The Wall Street Journal,* June 27, 1972; Richard Wightman, *Supermarket News,* April 2, 1973; Alice Zarillo, *Supermarket News,* March 26, 1973; interviews with A. Donald Seaborg and James Vermeer of the USDA Economic Research Service.

Sidney Margolius, *The Great American Food Hoax,* New York: Walker, 1971; Sylvia Porter column, June 23, 1972; John A. Prestbo, *The Wall Street Journal,* March 16, 1973; Spencer Rich, *The Washington Post,* March 20, 1973.

CHAPTER 11

George Dorsey, *The Washington Post,* December 31, 1972; Orville L. Freeman, *World Without Hunger,* New York: Praeger, 1968; Seth S. King, *The New York Times,* March 23, 1973; *The New York Times,* February 28, 1973; William and Paul Paddock, *Famine—1975!* Boston: Little, Brown, 1966; Katsuri Rangan, *The New York Times,* August 8 and December 17, 1972, and February 7 and April 29, 1973; Lewis M. Simons, *Washington Post,* November 27 and December 11, 1972, and March 30 and April 9, 1973; James P. Sterba, *The New York Times,* April 15, 1973; James Trager, *The Bellybook,* op. cit., and *The Foodbook,* op. cit.; Bernard Weinraub, *The New York Times,* February 20, 1973.

CHAPTER 12

Robert Alden, *The New York Times,* January 2, 1973; Kathleen Teltsch, *The New York Times,* November 15, 1972; interviews with John A. Schnittker and with Melvin Sjervin, *Milling & Baking News.*

Joseph Alsop columns, especially February 21, 1973; Marilyn Berger, *The Washington Post,* February 25, 1973; Tillman Durdin, *The New York Times,* January 2, 1973; Emily Hahn and the editors of Time-Life Books, *The Cooking of China,* New York: Time-Life

Books, 1968; William D. Hartley, *The Wall Street Journal*, August 31, 1970; Robert Keatley, *The Wall Street Journal*, July 7, 1971; Stanley Karnow, *Mao and China*, New York: Viking, 1972; Michell C. Lynch, *The Wall Street Journal*, July 19, 1971; *The New York Times*, June 11, 1972; Don Oberdorfer, *The Washington Post*, April 7, 1973; Warren H. Phillips, *The Wall Street Journal*, November 3 and December 20, 1972; Reuters News Agency, October 2, 1972; Harrison Salisbury, *The New York Times*, June 27, 1972; Willem F. Wertheim, *Ceres*, September–October, 1972; interview with Morton I. Sosland.

CHAPTER 13

Helen and George Papashvily and the editors of Time-Life Books, *Russian Cooking*, New York: Time-Life Books, 1971.

Mr. Hayward was quoted in Joseph Alsop's column, January 10, 1973; Stephens Broening, AP, January 29, 1973; James F. Clarity, *The New York Times*, July 4, 1970; Robert G. Kaiser, *The Washington Post*, March 13, 1973; Robert Keatley, *The Wall Street Journal*, April 10, 1973; Don Kendall, AP, *The Washington Post*, October 10, 1972; John Morrison, Reuters News Service, October 30, 1972; Reuters News Service, December 21, 1972; Charlotte Saikowski, Christian Science Monitor News Service, *The Washington Post*, August 24, 1972; Murray Seeger, *The Washington Post*, December 14, 1972; Theodore Shabad, *The New York Times*, September 25 and October 15, 1972, and April 23, 1973; Hedrick Smith, *The New York Times*, September 3 and 10, 1972, and February 4, 1973; *The Wall Street Journal*, September 10, 1972.

CHAPTER 14

Interview with Sheldon L. Berens; Nick Kotz, *The Washington Post*, November 14, 1972, and April 8, 1973; Reuters News Service, September 21, 1972.

Norman H. Fischer, *The Wall Street Journal*, February 6, 1973; Lewis M. Phelps, *The Wall Street Journal*, January 31, 1973; *The New York Times*, March 4, 1973.

CHAPTER 15

Nadine Brozan, *The New York Times*, January 11, 1973; Carl C. Craft, *The Washington Post*, March 9, 1972; Harold Faber, *The New York Times*, February 8, 1972; E. S. E. Hafez, *Reproduction in Farm Animals*, op. cit.; Burt Schorr, *The Wall Street Journal*, February 22, 1972; *Supermarket News*, February 26, 1973; *Time*, March 27, 1972; James Trager, *The Foodbook*, op. cit.; Robert A. Wright, *The New York Times*, April 8, 1972.

Tobi Nyborg, *Supermarket News,* March 12, 1973; Sylvia Porter column, August 10, 1972; *Supermarket News* (FNS), February 26, 1973; James Trager, *The Foodbook,* op. cit.; *The Washington Post* editorial, January 11, 1973.

CHAPTER 16

David Brand, *The Wall Street Journal,* September 8, 1972; David Joravsky, *The Lysenko Affair,* Cambridge: Harvard University Press, 1970; Zhores A. Medvedev, *The Rise and Fall of T. D. Lysenko,* Garden City, N.Y.: Doubleday Anchor, 1971; C. L. Sulzberger, *The New York Times,* June 7, 1970; interview with Morton I. Sosland; Mr. Butz was quoted in a Reuters News Service report, August 15, 1972.

CHAPTER 17

Norman H. Fischer, *The Wall Street Journal,* March 12, 1973; James P. Gannon, *The Wall Street Journal,* March 13, 1973; H. J. Maidenberg, *The New York Times,* February 28, March 4, March 14, and April 12, 1973; William Robbins, *The New York Times,* March 12, 1973; Burt Schorr, *The Wall Street Journal,* March 21, 1973; Robert A. Wright, *The New York Times,* February 19, 1973; interview with Morton I. Sosland.

John H. Allan, *The New York Times,* February 19, 1973; Clyde H. Farnsworth, *The New York Times,* May 8, 1973; Brandon Jones, *The New York Times,* February 14, 1973; William Robbins, *The New York Times,* February 27, 1973; Hobart Rowen, *The Washington Post,* March 29, 1973; Harrison Salisbury, *Russia,* op. cit.; interviews with John A. Schnittker and Morton I. Sosland.

CHAPTER 18

Lester R. Brown, *The Wall Street Journal,* March 26, 1973; Earl L. Butz, address to Chicago Mercantile Exchange, January 15, 1973; Hendrik S. Houthakker, *The Wall Street Journal,* January 16, 1973; David Mutch, Christian Science Monitor News Service, *The Washington Post,* March 11, 1973; *The New York Times,* December 7, 1971; John A. Prestbo, *The Wall Street Journal,* January 29, 1973; Francis I. Partsch, *The Wall Street Journal,* October 25, 1971; William Robbins, *The New York Times,* February 18 and March 21, 1973; Burt Schorr, *The Wall Street Journal,* January 16, 1973; Morton I. Sosland, address to Food Seminar for Institutional Investors, Minneapolis, February 6, 1973; Morton I. Sosland, *The New York Times,* March 11, 1973; George C. Wilson, *The Washington Post,* April 9, 1973.

INDEX